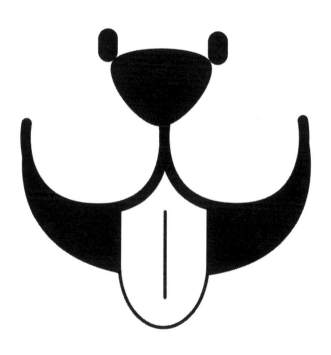

_____

_____

MUNROS TICK & LIST

☐	1	BEN NEVIS	1345M	4409 FT
☑	2	BEN MACDUI	1309M	4295 FT
☐	3	BRAERIACH	1296M	4252 FT
☐	4	CAIRN TOUL	1291M	4236 FT
☐	5	SGOR AN LOCHAIN UAINE	1258M	4127 FT
☐	6	CAIRN GORM	1245M	4081 FT
☐	7	AONACH BEAG (NEVIS RANGE)	1234M	4049 FT
☐	8	AONACH MOR	1221M	4006 FT
☐	9	CARN MOR DEARG	1220M	4003 FT
☐	10	BEN LAWERS	1214M	3983 FT
☐	11	BEINN A'BHUIRD	1197M	3927 FT
☐	12	CARN EIGE	1183M	3881 FT
☐	13	BEINN MHEADHOIN	1182M	3878 FT
☐	14	MAM SODHAIL	1181M	3875 FT
☐	15	STOB CHOIRE CLAURIGH	1177M	3862 FT
☐	16	BEN MORE	1174M	3852 FT
☐	17	BEN AVON	1171M	3842 FT
☐	18	STOB BINNEIN	1165M	3822 FT
☐	19	BEINN BHROTAIN	1157M	3796 FT
☑	20	DERRY CAIRNGORM	1155M	3789 FT
☑	21	LOCHNAGAR	1155M	3789 FT
☐	22	SGURR NAN CEATHREAMHNAN	1151M	3776 FT
☐	23	BIDEAN NAM BIAN	1150M	3773 FT
☐	24	SGURR NA LAPAICH	1150M	3773 FT
☐	25	BEN ALDER	1148M	3766 FT
☐	26	GEAL-CHARN (ALDER)	1132M	3741 FT
☐	27	BEN LUI	1130M	3707 FT
☐	28	BINNEIN MOR	1130M	3707 FT
☐	29	CREAG MEAGAIDH	1130M	3704 FT
☐	30	AN RIABHACHAN	1129M	3701 FT
☐	31	BEN CRUACHAN	1126M	3694 FT
☐	32	CARN NAN GABHAR	1121M	3678 FT
☐	33	A' CHRALAIG	1120M	3674 FT
☐	34	AN STUC	1118M	3668 FT
☐	35	CARN A'CHOIRE BHOIDHEACH	1118M	3668 FT
☐	36	MEALL GARBH (BEN LAWERS)	1118M	3668 FT
☐	37	SGOR GAOITH	1118M	3661 FT
☐	38	AONACH BEAG (ALDER)	1116M	3661 FT
☐	39	STOB COIRE AN LAOIGH	1116M	3658 FT
☐	40	STOB COIRE EASAIN	1115M	3652 FT
☐	41	MONADH MOR	1113M	3648 FT
☐	42	TOM A'CHOINICH	1112M	3642 FT
☐	43	SGURR MOR	1110M	3642 FT
☐	44	SGURR NAN CONBHAIREAN	1109M	3638 FT
☐	45	MEALL A'BHUIRIDH	1108M	3635 FT

❑ 46	STOB A'CHOIRE MHEADHOIN	1106M	3625 FT
❑ 47	BEINN GHLAS	1103M	3619 FT
❑ 48	BEINN EIBHINN	1102M	3615 FT
❑ 49	MULLACH FRAOCH-CHOIRE	1102M	3615 FT
❑ 50	CREISE	1100M	3609 FT
❑ 51	SGURR A'MHAIM	1099M	3606 FT
❑ 52	SGURR CHOINNICH MOR	1094M	3589 FT
❑ 53	SGURR NAN CLACH GEALA	1093M	3586 FT
❑ 54	BYNACK MORE	1090M	3576 FT
❑ 55	STOB GHABHAR	1090M	3576 FT
❑ 56	BEINN A'CHLACHAIR	1087M	3566 FT
❑ 57	BEINN DEARG (ULLAPOOL)	1084M	3556 FT
❑ 58	SCHIEHALLION	1083M	3553 FT
❑ 59	SGURR A'CHOIRE GHLAIS	1083M	3553 FT
❑ 60	BEINN A'CHAORAINN (CAIRNGORMS)	1082M	3553 FT
❑ 61	BEINN A'CHREACHAIN	1081M	3547 FT
❑ 62	BEINN HEASGARNICH	1078M	3537 FT
❑ 63	BEN STARAV	1078M	3537 FT
❑ 64	BEINN DORAIN	1076M	3530 FT
❑ 65	STOB COIRE SGREAMHACH	1072M	3517 FT
❑ 66	BRAIGH COIRE CHRUINN-BHALGAIN	1070M	3510 FT
❑ 67	AN SOCACH (MULLARDOCH)	1069M	3507 FT
❑ 68	MEALL CORRANAICH	1069M	3507 FT
❑ 69	GLAS MAOL	1068M	3504 FT
❑ 70	SGURR FHUARAN	1067M	3501 FT
❑ 71	CAIRN OF CLAISE	1064M	3491 FT
❑ 72	BIDEIN A'GHLAS THUILL (AN TEALLACH)	1062M	3484 FT
❑ 73	SGURR FIONA (AN TEALLACH)	1060M	3478 FT
❑ 74	NA GRUAGAICHEAN	1056M	3465 FT
❑ 75	SPIDEAN A'CHOIRE LEITH (LIATHACH)	1055M	3461 FT
❑ 76	STOB POITE COIRE ARDAIR	1054M	3458 FT
❑ 77	TOLL CREAGACH	1054M	3458 FT
❑ 78	SGURR A'CHAORACHAIN	1053M	3455 FT
❑ 79	GLAS TULAICHEAN	1051M	3448 FT
❑ 80	BEINN A'CHAORAINN (GLEN SPEAN)	1050M	3442 FT
❑ 81	GEAL CHARN	1049M	3442 FT
❑ 82	SGURR FHUAR-THUILL	1049M	3442 FT
❑ 83	CARN AN T-SAGAIRT MOR	1047M	3435 FT
❑ 84	CREAG MHOR (GLEN LOCHAY)	1047M	3435 FT
❑ 85	BEN WYVIS	1046M	3432 FT
❑ 86	CHNO DEARG	1046M	3432 FT
❑ 87	CRUACH ARDRAIN	1046M	3432 FT
❑ 88	BEINN IUTHARN MHOR	1045M	3428 FT
❑ 89	MEALL NAN TARMACHAN	1044M	3425 FT
❑ 90	STOB COIR AN ALBANNAICH	1044M	3425 FT

☐	91	CARN MAIRG	1042M	3415 FT
☐	92	SGURR NA CICHE	1040M	3412 FT
☐	93	MEALL GHAORDAIDH	1039M	3409 FT
☐	94	BEINN ACHALADAIR	1038M	3405 FT
☐	95	CARN A'MHAIM	1037M	3402 FT
☐	96	SGURR A'BHEALAICH DHEIRG	1036M	3399 FT
☐	97	GLEOURAICH	1035M	3396 FT
☐	98	CARN DEARG (LOCH PATTACK)	1034M	3392 FT
☐	99	AM BODACH	1032M	3386 FT
☐	100	BEINN FHADA	1032M	3386 FT
☐	101	BEN OSS	1029M	3376 FT
☐	102	CARN AN RIGH	1029M	3376 FT
☐	103	CARN GORM	1029M	3376 FT
☐	104	SGURR A'MHAORAICH	1027M	3369 FT
☐	105	SGURR NA CISTE DUIBHE	1027M	3369 FT
☐	106	BEN CHALLUM	1025M	3363 FT
☐	107	SGORR DHEARG (BEINN A'BHEITHIR)	1024M	3360 FT
☐	108	MULLACH AN RATHAIN (LIATHACH)	1023M	3356 FT
☐	109	AONACH AIR CHRITH	1021M	3350 FT
☐	110	STOB DEARG (BUACHAILLE ETIVE MOR)	1021M	3350 FT
☐	111	LADHAR BHEINN	1020M	3346 FT
☐	112	BEINN BHEOIL	1019M	3343 FT
☐	113	CARN AN TUIRC	1019M	3343 FT
☐	114	MULLACH CLACH A'BHLAIR	1019M	3343 FT
☐	115	MULLACH COIRE MHIC FHEARCHAIR	1019M	3340 FT
☐	116	GARBH CHIOCH MHOR	1013M	3323 FT
☐	117	CAIRN BANNOCH	1012M	3320 FT
☐	118	BEINN IME	1011M	3317 FT
☐	119	BEINN UDLAMAIN	1010M	3317 FT
☐	120	RUADH-STAC MOR (BEINN EIGHE)	1010M	3314 FT
☐	121	SGURR AN DOIRE LEATHAIN	1010M	3314 FT
☐	122	SGURR EILDE MOR	1010M	3314 FT
☐	123	THE SADDLE	1010M	3314 FT
☐	124	BEINN DEARG (BLAIR ATHOLL)	1008M	3307 FT
☐	125	MAOILE LUNNDAIDH	1007M	3304 FT
☐	126	AN SGARSOCH	1006M	3301 FT
☐	127	CARN LIATH (CREAG MEAGAIDH)	1006M	3301 FT
☐	128	BEINN FHIONNLAIDH (CARN EIGE)	1005M	3297 FT
☐	129	BEINN AN DOTHAIDH	1004M	3294 FT
☐	130	SGURR AN LOCHAIN	1004M	3294 FT
☐	131	THE DEVIL'S POINT	1004M	3294 FT
☐	132	SGURR MOR (LOCH QUOICH)	1003M	3291 FT
☐	133	SAIL CHAORAINN	1002M	3287 FT
☐	134	SGURR NA CARNACH	1002M	3287 FT
☐	135	AONACH MEADHOIN	1001M	3284 FT

❏ 136	MEALL GREIGH	1001M	3284 FT
❏ 137	SGORR DHONUILL (BEINN A'BHEITHIR)	1001M	3284 FT
❏ 138	SGURR BREAC	999M	3278 FT
❏ 139	SGURR CHOINNICH	999M	3278 FT
❏ 140	STOB BAN (MAMORES)	999M	3278 FT
❏ 141	BEN MORE ASSYNT	998M	3274 FT
❏ 142	BROAD CAIRN	998M	3274 FT
❏ 143	STOB DAIMH	998M	3274 FT
❏ 144	A' CHAILLEACH	997M	3271 FT
❏ 145	GLAS BHEINN MHOR	997M	3271 FT
❏ 146	SPIDEAN MIALACH	996M	3268 FT
❏ 147	AN CAISTEAL	995M	3264 FT
❏ 148	CARN AN FHIDHLEIR (CARN EALAR)	994M	3261 FT
❏ 149	SGOR NA H-ULAIDH	994M	3261 FT
❏ 150	SGURR NA RUAIDHE	993M	3258 FT
❏ 151	SPIDEAN COIRE NAN CLACH (BEINN EIGHE)	993M	3258 FT
❏ 152	CARN NAN GOBHAR (LOCH MULLARDOCH)	992M	3255 FT
❏ 153	CARN NAN GOBHAR (STRATHFARRAR)	992M	3255 FT
❏ 154	SGURR ALASDAIR	992M	3255 FT
❏ 155	SGAIRNEACH MHOR	991M	3251 FT
❏ 156	BEINN EUNAICH	989M	3245 FT
❏ 157	SGURR BAN	989M	3245 FT
❏ 158	CONIVAL	987M	3238 FT
❏ 159	CREAG LEACACH	987M	3238 FT
❏ 160	DRUIM SHIONNACH	987M	3238 FT
❏ 161	GULVAIN	987M	3238 FT
❏ 162	INACCESSIBLE PINNACLE	986M	3235 FT
❏ 163	LURG MHOR	986M	3235 FT
❏ 164	SGURR MOR (BEINN ALLIGIN)	986M	3235 FT
❏ 165	BEN VORLICH (LOCH EARN)	985M	3232 FT
❏ 166	AN GEARANACH	982M	3222 FT
❏ 167	MULLACH NAN DHEIRAGAIN	982M	3222 FT
❏ 168	CREAG MHOR (MEALL NA AIGHEAN)	981M	3218 FT
❏ 169	MAOL CHINN-DEARG	981M	3218 FT
❏ 170	SLIOCH	981M	3218 FT
❏ 171	STOB COIRE A'CHAIRN	981M	3218 FT
❏ 172	BEINN A'CHOCHUILL	980M	3215 FT
❏ 173	CISTE DHUBH	979M	3212 FT
❏ 174	STOB COIRE SGRIODAIN	979M	3212 FT
❏ 175	BEINN DUBHCHRAIG	978M	3209 FT
❏ 176	CONA' MHEALL	978M	3209 FT
❏ 177	MEALL NAN CEAPRAICHEAN	977M	3205 FT
❏ 178	STOB BAN (GREY CORRIES)	977M	3205 FT
❏ 179	A' MHARCONAICH	975M	3199 FT
❏ 180	CARN A'GHEOIDH	975M	3199 FT

☐	181	CARN LIATH (BEINN A'GHLO)	975M	3199 FT
☐	182	STUC A'CHROIN	975M	3199 FT
☐	183	BEINN SGRITHEALL	974M	3195 FT
☐	184	BEN LOMOND	974M	3195 FT
☐	185	SGURR A'GHREADAIDH	973M	3192 FT
☐	186	MEALL GARBH (CARN MAIRG)	968M	3176 FT
☐	187	A' MHAIGHDEAN	967M	3173 FT
☐	188	SGORR NAM FIANNAIDH (AONACH EAGACH)	967M	3173 FT
☐	189	BEN MORE (MULL)	966M	3169 FT
☐	190	SGURR NA BANACHDICH	965M	3166 FT
☐	191	SGURR NAN GILLEAN	964M	3162 FT
☐	192	CARN A'CHLAMAIN	963M	3159 FT
☐	193	SGURR THUILM	963M	3159 FT
☐	194	SGORR RUADH	962M	3156 FT
☐	195	BEN KLIBRECK	961M	3156 FT
☐	196	BEINN NAN AIGHENAN	960M	3150 FT
☐	197	STUCHD AN LOCHAIN	960M	3150 FT
☐	198	BEINN FHIONNLAIDH	959M	3146 FT
☐	199	MEALL GLAS	959M	3146 FT
☐	200	BRUACH NA FRITHE	958M	3143 FT
☐	201	TOLMOUNT	958M	3143 FT
☐	202	CARN GHLUASAID	957M	3143 FT
☐	203	TOM BUIDHE	957M	3140 FT
☐	204	SAILEAG	956M	3140 FT
☐	205	SGURR NAN COIREACHAN (GLENFINNAN)	956M	3136 FT
☐	206	STOB DUBH (BUACHAILLE ETIVE BEAG)	956M	3136 FT
☐	207	STOB NA BROIGE (BUACHAILLE ETIVE MOR)	956M	3136 FT
☐	208	SGOR GAIBHRE	955M	3133 FT
☐	209	AM FAOCHAGACH	954M	3130 FT
☐	210	BEINN LIATH MHOR FANNAICH	954M	3130 FT
☐	211	BEINN MHANACH	953M	3130 FT
☐	212	MEALL DEARG (AONACH EAGACH)	953M	3127 FT
☐	*213	SGURR NAN COIREACHAN (GLEN DESSARY)	953M	3127 FT
☐	214	MEALL CHUAICH	951M	3120 FT
☐	215	MEALL GORM	949M	3113 FT
☐	216	BEINN BHUIDHE	948M	3110 FT
☐	217	SGURR MHIC CHOINNICH	948M	3110 FT
☐	218	CREAG A'MHAIM	947M	3107 FT
☐	219	DRIESH	947M	3107 FT
☐	220	BEINN TULAICHEAN	946M	3104 FT
☐	221	CARN BHAC	946M	3104 FT
☐	222	MEALL BUIDHE (KNOYDART)	94CM	3104 FT
☐	223	BIDEIN A'CHOIRE SHEASGAICH	945M	3104 FT
☐	224	CARN DEARG (MONADHLIATH)	945M	3100 FT
☐	225	SGURR NA SGINE	945M	3100 FT

❑ 226	STOB A'CHOIRE ODHAIR	945M	3100 FT
❑ 227	AN SOCACH (BRAEMAR)	944M	3097 FT
❑ 228	SGURR DUBH MOR	944M	3097 FT
❑ 229	BEN VORLICH (LOCH LOMOND)	943M	3094 FT
❑ 230	BINNEIN BEAG	943M	3094 FT
❑ 231	BEINN A'CHROIN	942M	3087 FT
❑ 232	CARN DEARG (CORROUR)	941M	3087 FT
❑ 233	CARN NA CAIM	941M	3084 FT
❑ 234	LUINNE BHEINN	939M	3081 FT
❑ 235	MOUNT KEEN	939M	3081 FT
❑ 236	MULLACH NAN COIREAN	939M	3081 FT
❑ 237	BEINN NA LAP	937M	3074 FT
❑ 238	BEINN SGULAIRD	937M	3071 FT
❑ 239	BEINN TARSUINN	937M	3071 FT
❑ 240	SRON A'CHOIRE GHAIRBH	937M	3071 FT
❑ 241	A' BHUIDHEANACH BHEAG	936M	3068 FT
❑ 242	AM BASTEIR	934M	3064 FT
❑ 243	MEALL A'CHRASGAIDH	934M	3064 FT
❑ 244	BEINN CHABHAIR	933M	3061 FT
❑ 245	FIONN BHEINN	933M	3061 FT
❑ 246	MAOL CHEAN-DEARG	933M	3061 FT
❑ 247	THE CAIRNWELL	933M	3061 FT
❑ 248	MEALL BUIDHE (GLEN LYON)	932M	3058 FT
❑ 249	BEINN BHREAC	931M	3054 FT
❑ 250	BEN CHONZIE	931M	3054 FT
❑ 251	A' CHAILLEACH (MONADHLIATH)	930M	3051 FT
❑ 252	BLA BHEINN	928M	3045 FT
❑ 253	MAYAR	928M	3045 FT
❑ 254	MEALL NAN EUN	928M	3045 FT
❑ 255	MORUISG	928M	3045 FT
❑ 256	BEN HOPE	927M	3041 FT
❑ 257	EIDIDH NAN CLACH GEALA	927M	3041 FT
❑ 258	BEINN LIATH MHOR	926M	3038 FT
❑ 259	BEINN NARNAIN	926M	3038 FT
❑ 260	GEAL CHARN (MONADHLIATH)	926M	3038 FT
❑ 261	MEALL A'CHOIRE LEITH	926M	3038 FT
❑ 262	SEANA BHRAIGH	926M	3038 FT
❑ 263	STOB COIRE RAINEACH	925M	3035 FT
❑ 264	CREAG PITRIDH	924M	3031 FT
❑ 265	SGURR NAN EAG	924M	3031 FT
❑ 266	AN COILEACHAN	923M	3028 FT
❑ 267	SGURR NAN EACH	923M	3028 FT
❑ 268	TOM NA GRUAGAICH	922M	3025 FT
❑ 269	AN SOCACH (AFFRIC)	921M	3022 FT
❑ 270	SGIATH CHUIL	921M	3022 FT

☐ 271	CARN SGULAIN	920M	3018 FT
☐ 272	GAIRICH	919M	3015 FT
☐ 273	A' GHLAS-BHEINN	918M	3012 FT
☐ 274	CREAG NAN DAMH	918M	3012 FT
☐ 275	MEALL NA TEANGA	918M	3012 FT
☐ 276	RUADH STAC MOR	918M	3012 FT
☐ 277	SGURR A'MHADAIDH	918M	3012 FT
☐ 278	CARN AOSDA	917M	3008 FT
☐ 279	GEAL-CHARN (DRUMOCHTER)	917M	3008 FT
☐ 280	BEINN A'CHLEIBH	916M	3005 FT
☐ 281	BEINN TEALLACH	915M	3002 FT
☐ 282	BEN VANE	915M	3002 FT

DRIESH

"THE THORN BUSH"

ANGUS	947M

DATE:	DISTANCE:	
WEATHER:	PEE	POO
TIME TAKEN:	ENJOYABLE ☆☆☆	

NOTES/PHOTOGRAPH/KEEP SAKE:

_____

_____

_____

_____

_____

_____

_____

_____

_____

_____

_____

_____

_____

_____

MAYAR

"THE OBSCURE HILL"

ANGUS		928M

DATE:	DISTANCE:	
WEATHER:	PEE	POO
TIME TAKEN:	**ENJOYABLE** ☆☆☆	

NOTES/PHOTOGRAPH/KEEP SAKE:

_____

_____

_____

_____

_____

_____

_____

_____

_____

_____

_____

_____

_____

MOUNT KEEN

"THE GENTLE HILL"

ANGUS	939M

DATE:	DISTANCE:	
WEATHER:	PEE	POO
TIME TAKEN:	**ENJOYABLE** ☆☆☆	

NOTES/PHOTOGRAPH/KEEP SAKE:

_____

_____

_____

_____

_____

_____

_____

_____

_____

_____

_____

_____

_____

_____

_____

_____

BEINN A'CHLEIBH

"THE HILL OF THE CHEST"

ARGYLL		916M	
DATE:	DISTANCE:		
WEATHER:	PEE		POO
TIME TAKEN:	ENJOYABLE ☆☆☆		

NOTES/PHOTOGRAPH/KEEP SAKE:

_____

_____

_____

_____

_____

_____

_____

_____

_____

_____

_____

_____

_____

BEINN A'CHOCHUILL

"THE HILL OF THE SHELL"

ARGYLL	980M

DATE:	DISTANCE:	
WEATHER:	**PEE**	**POO**
TIME TAKEN:	**ENJOYABLE** ☆ ☆ ☆	

NOTES/PHOTOGRAPH/KEEP SAKE:

_____

_____

_____

_____

_____

_____

_____

_____

_____

_____

_____

_____

_____

BEINN A'CHREACHAIN

"THE MOUNTAIN OF THE BARE ROCK"

ARGYLL	1081M

DATE:	DISTANCE:	
WEATHER:	PEE	POO
TIME TAKEN:	ENJOYABLE ☆☆☆	

NOTES/PHOTOGRAPH/KEEP SAKE:

_____
_____
_____
_____
_____
_____
_____
_____
_____
_____
_____
_____
_____

BEINN ACHALADAIR

"THE HILL OF THE FIELD BY THE HARD WATER"

ARGYLL   **1038M**

DATE:	DISTANCE:	
WEATHER:	**PEE**	**POO**
TIME TAKEN:	**ENJOYABLE** ☆☆☆	

NOTES/PHOTOGRAPH/KEEP SAKE:

_____

_____

_____

_____

_____

_____

_____

_____

_____

_____

_____

_____

_____

BEINN AN DOTHAIDH

"THE HILL OF THE SCORCHING"

ARGYLL		1004M	
DATE:	DISTANCE:		
WEATHER:		PEE	POO
TIME TAKEN:	ENJOYABLE ☆ ☆ ☆		

NOTES/PHOTOGRAPH/KEEP SAKE:

_____

_____

_____

_____

_____

_____

_____

_____

_____

_____

_____

_____

BEINN BHUIDHE

"THE YELLOW HILL"

ARGYLL   948M

DATE:	DISTANCE:	
WEATHER:	PEE	POO
TIME TAKEN:	ENJOYABLE ☆☆☆	

NOTES/PHOTOGRAPH/KEEP SAKE:

_____

_____

_____

_____

_____

_____

_____

_____

_____

_____

_____

_____

_____

_____

BEINN DORAIN

"THE HILL OF THE STREAMLET"

ARGYLL		1076M

DATE:	DISTANCE:	
WEATHER:	PEE	POO
TIME TAKEN:	ENJOYABLE ☆☆☆	

NOTES/PHOTOGRAPH/KEEP SAKE:

_____
_____
_____
_____
_____
_____
_____
_____
_____
_____
_____
_____
_____

BEINN DUBHCHRAIG

"THE MOUNTAIN OF THE BLACK ROCK"

ARGYLL   978M

DATE:	DISTANCE:	
WEATHER:	PEE	POO
TIME TAKEN:	ENJOYABLE ☆☆☆	

NOTES/PHOTOGRAPH/KEEP SAKE:

_____

_____

_____

_____

_____

_____

_____

_____

_____

_____

_____

_____

_____

_____

BEINN EUNAICH

"THE FOWLING HILL"

ARGYLL   989M

DATE:	DISTANCE:		
WEATHER:		PEE	POO
TIME TAKEN:	ENJOYABLE ☆☆☆		

NOTES/PHOTOGRAPH/KEEP SAKE:

_____
_____
_____
_____
_____
_____
_____
_____
_____
_____
_____
_____
_____

BEINN FHIONNLAIDH

"THE FINDLAY'S HILL"

ARGYLL		959M	
DATE:	**DISTANCE:**		
WEATHER:	**PEE**		**POO**
TIME TAKEN:	**ENJOYABLE** ☆☆☆		

NOTES/PHOTOGRAPH/KEEP SAKE:

_____

_____

_____

_____

_____

_____

_____

_____

_____

_____

_____

_____

_____

BEINN MHANACH

"THE MONK'S HILL"

ARGYLL	953M

DATE:	DISTANCE:	
WEATHER:	PEE	POO
TIME TAKEN:	**ENJOYABLE** ☆☆☆	

NOTES/PHOTOGRAPH/KEEP SAKE:

_____

_____

_____

_____

_____

_____

_____

_____

_____

_____

_____

_____

_____

BEINN SGULAIRD

"THE HAT SHAPED HILL"

ARGYLL		937M

DATE:	DISTANCE:	
WEATHER:	**PEE**	**POO**
TIME TAKEN:	**ENJOYABLE** ☆☆☆	

NOTES/PHOTOGRAPH/KEEP SAKE:

_____
_____
_____
_____
_____
_____
_____
_____
_____
_____
_____
_____
_____
_____

BEN CHALLUM

"THE MALCOLM'S HILL"

ARGYLL   1025M

DATE:	DISTANCE:	
WEATHER:	PEE	POO
TIME TAKEN:	**ENJOYABLE** ☆☆☆	

NOTES/PHOTOGRAPH/KEEP SAKE:

_____
_____
_____
_____
_____
_____
_____
_____
_____
_____
_____
_____
_____

BEN CRUACHAN

"THE STACKED HILL"

ARGYLL   1126M

DATE:	DISTANCE:	
WEATHER:	PEE	POO
TIME TAKEN:	ENJOYABLE ☆☆☆	

NOTES/PHOTOGRAPH/KEEP SAKE:

_____

_____

_____

_____

_____

_____

_____

_____

_____

_____

_____

_____

_____

_____

BEN LUI

"THE HILL OF THE CALF"

ARGYLL		1130M

DATE:	DISTANCE:	
WEATHER:	PEE	POO
TIME TAKEN:	ENJOYABLE ☆☆☆	

NOTES/PHOTOGRAPH/KEEP SAKE:

_____
_____
_____
_____
_____
_____
_____
_____
_____
_____
_____
_____
_____

BEN OSS

"THE MOUNTAIN OF THE ELK"

ARGYLL	1029M

DATE:	DISTANCE:	
WEATHER:	PEE	POO
TIME TAKEN:	ENJOYABLE ☆☆☆	

NOTES/PHOTOGRAPH/KEEP SAKE:

_____

_____

_____

_____

_____

_____

_____

_____

_____

_____

_____

_____

_____

STOB A'CHOIRE ODHAIR

"THE PEAK OF THE DAPPLED CORRIE"

ARGYLL	945M

DATE:	DISTANCE:	
WEATHER:	PEE	POO
TIME TAKEN:	ENJOYABLE ☆☆☆	

NOTES/PHOTOGRAPH/KEEP SAKE:

_____
_____
_____
_____
_____
_____
_____
_____
_____
_____
_____
_____

STOB DAIMH

"THE PEAK OF THE STAG"

ARGYLL	998M

DATE:	DISTANCE:	
WEATHER:	**PEE**	**POO**
TIME TAKEN:	**ENJOYABLE** ☆☆☆	

NOTES/PHOTOGRAPH/KEEP SAKE:

_____

_____

_____

_____

_____

_____

_____

_____

_____

_____

_____

_____

_____

STOB GHABHAR

"THE PEAK OF THE GOATS"

ARGYLL	1090M

DATE:	DISTANCE:	
WEATHER:	PEE	POO
TIME TAKEN:	ENJOYABLE ☆☆☆	

NOTES/PHOTOGRAPH/KEEP SAKE:

_____
_____
_____
_____
_____
_____
_____
_____
_____
_____
_____
_____

A' BHUIDHEANACH BHEAG

"THE LITTLE YELLOW PLACE"

CAIRNGORMS   936M

DATE:	DISTANCE:	
WEATHER:	PEE	POO
TIME TAKEN:	ENJOYABLE ☆☆☆	

NOTES/PHOTOGRAPH/KEEP SAKE:

_____
_____
_____
_____
_____
_____
_____
_____
_____
_____
_____
_____
_____
_____

A' CHAILLEACH (MONADHLIATH)

"THE OLD WOMAN"

CAIRNGORMS   930M

DATE:	DISTANCE:	
WEATHER:	PEE	POO
TIME TAKEN:	ENJOYABLE ☆☆☆	

NOTES/PHOTOGRAPH/KEEP SAKE:

_____
_____
_____
_____
_____
_____
_____
_____
_____
_____
_____
_____
_____

A' MHARCONAICH

"THE PLACE OF THE HORSE"

CAIRNGORMS	975M

DATE:	DISTANCE:	
WEATHER:	**PEE**	**POO**
TIME TAKEN:	**ENJOYABLE** ☆☆☆	

NOTES/PHOTOGRAPH/KEEP SAKE:

_____
_____
_____
_____
_____
_____
_____
_____
_____
_____
_____
_____
_____
_____

AN SGARSOCH

"THE PLACE OF SHARP ROCKS"

CAIRNGORMS		1006M

DATE:	DISTANCE:	
WEATHER:	PEE	POO
TIME TAKEN:	ENJOYABLE ☆☆☆	

NOTES/PHOTOGRAPH/KEEP SAKE:

_____
_____
_____
_____
_____
_____
_____
_____
_____
_____
_____
_____
_____

AN SOCACH (BRAEMAR)

"THE SNOUT"

CAIRNGORMS	944M

DATE:	DISTANCE:	
WEATHER:	**PEE**	**POO**
TIME TAKEN:	**ENJOYABLE** ☆☆☆	

NOTES/PHOTOGRAPH/KEEP SAKE:

_____

_____

_____

_____

_____

_____

_____

_____

_____

_____

_____

_____

_____

AONACH BEAG(ALDER)

"THE SMALL RIDGE"

CAIRNGORMS   1116M

DATE:	DISTANCE:	
WEATHER:	PEE	POO
TIME TAKEN:	**ENJOYABLE** ☆☆☆	

NOTES/PHOTOGRAPH/KEEP SAKE:

_____
_____
_____
_____
_____
_____
_____
_____
_____
_____
_____
_____

BEINN A'BHUIRD

"THE MOUNTAIN OF THE TABLE"

CAIRNGORMS   1197M

DATE:	DISTANCE:	
WEATHER:	PEE	POO
TIME TAKEN:	ENesetAStateToProps...	

DATE:	DISTANCE:	

NOTES/PHOTOGRAPH/KEEP SAKE:

_____
_____
_____
_____
_____
_____
_____
_____
_____
_____
_____
_____
_____
_____

BEINN A'CHAORAINN (CAIRNGORMS)

"THE HILL OF ROWAN"

CAIRNGORMS   1082M

DATE:	DISTANCE:	
WEATHER:	PEE	POO
TIME TAKEN:	ENJOYABLE ☆☆☆	

NOTES/PHOTOGRAPH/KEEP SAKE:

_____

_____

_____

_____

_____

_____

_____

_____

_____

_____

_____

_____

_____

BEINN BHEOIL

"THE HILL OF THE MOUTH"

CAIRNGORMS   1019M

DATE:	DISTANCE:	

WEATHER:	PEE	POO

TIME TAKEN:	ENJOYABLE ☆☆☆

NOTES/PHOTOGRAPH/KEEP SAKE:

_____
_____
_____
_____
_____
_____
_____
_____
_____
_____
_____
_____
_____

BEINN BHREAC

"THE SPECKLED HILL"

CAIRNGORMS	931M

DATE:	DISTANCE:	
WEATHER:	PEE	POO
TIME TAKEN:	ENJOYABLE ☆☆☆	

NOTES/PHOTOGRAPH/KEEP SAKE:

_____

_____

_____

_____

_____

_____

_____

_____

_____

_____

_____

_____

BEINN BHROTAIN

"THE HILL OF THE MASTIFF"

CAIRNGORMS		1157M

DATE:	DISTANCE:	
WEATHER:	**PEE**	**POO**
TIME TAKEN:	**ENJOYABLE** ☆☆☆	

NOTES/PHOTOGRAPH/KEEP SAKE:

_____
_____
_____
_____
_____
_____
_____
_____
_____
_____
_____
_____
_____
_____

BEINN EIBHINN

"THE DELIGHTFUL HILL"

CAIRNGORMS   1102M

DATE:	DISTANCE:	
WEATHER:	PEE	POO
TIME TAKEN:	**ENJOYABLE** ☆☆☆	

NOTES/PHOTOGRAPH/KEEP SAKE:

_____

_____

_____

_____

_____

_____

_____

_____

_____

_____

_____

_____

_____

BEINN IUTHARN MHOR

"THE BIG SHARP RIDGED HILL"

CAIRNGORMS   1045M

DATE:	DISTANCE:	
WEATHER:	PEE	POO
TIME TAKEN:	ENJOYABLE ☆☆☆	

NOTES/PHOTOGRAPH/KEEP SAKE:

_____

_____

_____

_____

_____

_____

_____

_____

_____

_____

_____

_____

_____

BEINN MHEADHOIN

"THE MIDDLE HILL"

CAIRNGORMS   1182M

DATE:	DISTANCE:	
WEATHER:	PEE	POO
TIME TAKEN:	ENJOYABLE ☆☆☆	

NOTES/PHOTOGRAPH/KEEP SAKE:

_____

_____

_____

_____

_____

_____

_____

_____

_____

_____

_____

_____

_____

BEINN UDLAMAIN

"THE GLOOMY HILL"

CAIRNGORMS   1010M

DATE:	DISTANCE:		
WEATHER:		PEE	POO
TIME TAKEN:	ENJOYABLE ☆☆☆		

NOTES/PHOTOGRAPH/KEEP SAKE:

_____

_____

_____

_____

_____

_____

_____

_____

_____

_____

_____

_____

_____

BEN ALDER

"THE HILL OF ROCK AND WATER"

CAIRNGORMS		1148M

DATE:	DISTANCE:	
WEATHER:	PEE	POO
TIME TAKEN:	ENJOYABLE ☆☆☆	

NOTES/PHOTOGRAPH/KEEP SAKE:

_____
_____
_____
_____
_____
_____
_____
_____
_____
_____
_____
_____
_____

BEN AVON

"THE HILL OF THE BRIGHT ONE"

CAIRNGORMS   1171M

DATE:	DISTANCE:	
WEATHER:	PEE	POO
TIME TAKEN:	ENJOYABLE ☆☆☆	

NOTES/PHOTOGRAPH/KEEP SAKE:

_____

_____

_____

_____

_____

_____

_____

_____

_____

_____

_____

_____

_____

BEN MACDUI

"THE HILL OF THE BLACK PIG"

CAIRNGORMS		1309M	
DATE:	**DISTANCE:**		
WEATHER:		**PEE**	**POO**
TIME TAKEN:	**ENJOYABLE** ☆ ☆ ☆		

NOTES/PHOTOGRAPH/KEEP SAKE:

_____

_____

_____

_____

_____

_____

_____

_____

_____

_____

_____

_____

_____

BRAERIACH

"THE GREY UPPER PART"

CAIRNGORMS	1296M

DATE:	DISTANCE:	
WEATHER:	PEE	POO
TIME TAKEN:	**ENJOYABLE** ☆☆☆	

NOTES/PHOTOGRAPH/KEEP SAKE:

_____
_____
_____
_____
_____
_____
_____
_____
_____
_____
_____
_____
_____

BROAD CAIRN

"THE BROAD CAIRN LIKE HIL"

CAIRNGORMS		998M

DATE:	DISTANCE:	
WEATHER:	PEE	POO
TIME TAKEN:	ENJOYABLE ☆☆☆	

NOTES/PHOTOGRAPH/KEEP SAKE:

_____
_____
_____
_____
_____
_____
_____
_____
_____
_____
_____
_____

BYNACK MORE

"THE BIG CAP"

CAIRNGORMS   1090M

DATE:	DISTANCE:	
WEATHER:	PEE	POO
TIME TAKEN:	ENJOYABLE ☆☆☆	

NOTES/PHOTOGRAPH/KEEP SAKE:

_____
_____
_____
_____
_____
_____
_____
_____
_____
_____
_____
_____
_____

CAIRN BANNOCH

"THE CAIRN LIKE HILL OF THE CAKE"

CAIRNGORMS   1012M

DATE:	DISTANCE:		
WEATHER:		PEE	POO
TIME TAKEN:	ENJOYABLE ☆☆☆		

NOTES/PHOTOGRAPH/KEEP SAKE:

_____

_____

_____

_____

_____

_____

_____

_____

_____

_____

_____

_____

CAIRN GORM

"THE BLUE CAIRN LIKE PEAK"

CAIRNGORMS   1245M

DATE:	DISTANCE:	
WEATHER:	PEE	POO
TIME TAKEN:	**ENJOYABLE** ☆☆☆	

NOTES/PHOTOGRAPH/KEEP SAKE:

_____

_____

_____

_____

_____

_____

_____

_____

_____

_____

_____

_____

_____

CAIRN OF CLAISE

"THE CAIRN LIKE PEAK OF THE GRASSY HOLLOW"

CAIRNGORMS   1064M

DATE:	DISTANCE:	
WEATHER:	PEE	POO
TIME TAKEN:	ENJOYABLE ☆☆☆	

NOTES/PHOTOGRAPH/KEEP SAKE:

_____
_____
_____
_____
_____
_____
_____
_____
_____
_____
_____
_____
_____

CAIRN TOUL

"THE HILL OF THE BARN"

CAIRNGORMS		1291M	
DATE:	**DISTANCE:**		
WEATHER:		PEE	POO
TIME TAKEN:	**ENJOYABLE** ☆☆☆		

NOTES/PHOTOGRAPH/KEEP SAKE:

_____

_____

_____

_____

_____

_____

_____

_____

_____

_____

_____

_____

_____

CARN A'CHOIRE BHOIDHEACH

"THE PEAK OF THE BEAUTIFUL CORRIE"

CAIRNGORMS   1118M

DATE:	DISTANCE:	
WEATHER:	PEE	POO
TIME TAKEN:	ENJOYABLE ☆☆☆	

NOTES/PHOTOGRAPH/KEEP SAKE:

_____
_____
_____
_____
_____
_____
_____
_____
_____
_____
_____
_____
_____

CARN A'GHEOIDH

"THE CAIRN LIKE PEAK OF THE GOOSE"

CAIRNGORMS   975M

DATE:	DISTANCE:	
WEATHER:	**PEE**	**POO**
TIME TAKEN:	**ENJOYABLE** ☆☆☆	

NOTES/PHOTOGRAPH/KEEP SAKE:

_____
_____
_____
_____
_____
_____
_____
_____
_____
_____
_____
_____
_____
_____

CARN A'MHAIM

"THE CAIRN LIKE PEAK OF THE LARGE ROUNDED HILL"

CAIRNGORMS   1037M

DATE:	DISTANCE:	
WEATHER:	PEE	POO
TIME TAKEN:	ENJOYABLE ☆☆☆	

NOTES/PHOTOGRAPH/KEEP SAKE:

_____
_____
_____
_____
_____
_____
_____
_____
_____
_____
_____
_____
_____

CARN AN FHIDHLEIR (CARN EALAR)

"THE CAIRN LIKE PEAK OF THE FIDDLER"

CAIRNGORMS   994M

DATE:	DISTANCE:	
WEATHER:	**PEE**	**POO**
TIME TAKEN:	**ENJOYABLE** ☆☆☆	

NOTES/PHOTOGRAPH/KEEP SAKE:

_____
_____
_____
_____
_____
_____
_____
_____
_____
_____
_____
_____
_____
_____

CARN AN T-SAGAIRT MOR

"THE BIG PEAK OF THE PRIEST"

CAIRNGORMS		1047M	
DATE:	DISTANCE:		
WEATHER:	PEE	POO	
TIME TAKEN:	ENJOYABLE ☆☆☆		

NOTES/PHOTOGRAPH/KEEP SAKE:

_____

_____

_____

_____

_____

_____

_____

_____

_____

_____

_____

_____

_____

_____

CARN AN TUIRC

"THE CAIRN LIKE PEAK OF THE WILD BOAR"

CAIRNGORMS   1019M

DATE:	DISTANCE:	
WEATHER:	PEE	POO
TIME TAKEN:	**ENJOYABLE** ☆☆☆	

NOTES/PHOTOGRAPH/KEEP SAKE:

_____

_____

_____

_____

_____

_____

_____

_____

_____

_____

_____

_____

_____

_____

CARN AOSDA

"THE ANCIENT PEAK"

CAIRNGORMS	917M

DATE:	DISTANCE:	
WEATHER:	PEE	POO
TIME TAKEN:	**ENJOYABLE** ☆☆☆	

NOTES/PHOTOGRAPH/KEEP SAKE:

_____

_____

_____

_____

_____

_____

_____

_____

_____

_____

_____

_____

CARN BHAC

"THE PEAK OF THE PEAT BANKS"

CAIRNGORMS	946M

DATE:	DISTANCE:	
WEATHER:	**PEE**	**POO**
TIME TAKEN:	**ENJOYABLE** ☆☆☆	

NOTES/PHOTOGRAPH/KEEP SAKE:

_____
_____
_____
_____
_____
_____
_____
_____
_____
_____
_____
_____
_____

CARN DEARG (LOCH PATTACK)

"THE RED CAIRN LIKE PEAK"

CAIRNGORMS 1034M

DATE:	DISTANCE:	
WEATHER:	PEE	POO
TIME TAKEN:	ENJOYABLE ☆☆☆	

NOTES/PHOTOGRAPH/KEEP SAKE:

_____
_____
_____
_____
_____
_____
_____
_____
_____
_____
_____
_____
_____

CARN DEARG (MONADHLIATH)

"THE RED CAIRN LIKE PEAK"

CAIRNGORMS   945M

DATE:	DISTANCE:	
WEATHER:	PEE	POO
TIME TAKEN:	ENJOYABLE ☆☆☆	

NOTES/PHOTOGRAPH/KEEP SAKE:

_____
_____
_____
_____
_____
_____
_____
_____
_____
_____
_____
_____
_____

CARN NA CAIM

"THE CAIRN LIKE PEAK OF THE CURVE"

CAIRNGORMS		941M

DATE:	DISTANCE:	
WEATHER:	PEE	POO
TIME TAKEN:	**ENJOYABLE** ☆☆☆	

NOTES/PHOTOGRAPH/KEEP SAKE:

_____
_____
_____
_____
_____
_____
_____
_____
_____
_____
_____
_____

CARN SGULAIN

"THE CAIRN LIKE PEAK OF THE BASKET"

CAIRNGORMS   920M

DATE:	DISTANCE:	
WEATHER:	PEE	POO
TIME TAKEN:	ENJOYABLE ☆☆☆	

NOTES/PHOTOGRAPH/KEEP SAKE:

_____
_____
_____
_____
_____
_____
_____
_____
_____
_____
_____
_____
_____
_____

CREAG LEACACH

"THE SLABBY CRAG"

CAIRNGORMS		987M

DATE:	DISTANCE:	
WEATHER:	**PEE**	**POO**
TIME TAKEN:	**ENJOYABLE** ☆☆☆	

NOTES/PHOTOGRAPH/KEEP SAKE:

_____

_____

_____

_____

_____

_____

_____

_____

_____

_____

_____

_____

_____

DERRY CAIRNGORM

"THE BLUE PEAK OF GLEN DERRY"

DATE:	DISTANCE:	
WEATHER:	PEE	POO
TIME TAKEN:	ENJOYABLE ☆☆☆	

NOTES/PHOTOGRAPH/KEEP SAKE:

_____

_____

_____

_____

_____

_____

_____

_____

_____

_____

_____

_____

_____

GEAL CHARN (MONADHLIATH)

"THE WHITE PEAK"

CAIRNGORMS	926M	
DATE:	DISTANCE:	
WEATHER:	PEE	POO
TIME TAKEN:	ENJOYABLE ☆☆☆	

NOTES/PHOTOGRAPH/KEEP SAKE:

_____

_____

_____

_____

_____

_____

_____

_____

_____

_____

_____

_____

GEAL-CHARN (ALDER)
"THE WHITE PEAK"

CAIRNGORMS   1132M

DATE:	DISTANCE:	
WEATHER:	PEE	POO
TIME TAKEN:	ENJOYABLE ☆☆☆	

NOTES/PHOTOGRAPH/KEEP SAKE:

_____
_____
_____
_____
_____
_____
_____
_____
_____
_____
_____
_____
_____
_____

GEAL-CHARN (DRUMOCHTER)

"THE WHITE PEAK"

CAIRNGORMS		917M

DATE:	DISTANCE:	
WEATHER:	PEE	POO
TIME TAKEN:	ENJOYABLE ☆☆☆	

NOTES/PHOTOGRAPH/KEEP SAKE:

_____
_____
_____
_____
_____
_____
_____
_____
_____
_____
_____
_____
_____

GLAS MAOL

"THE GREY-GREEN HILL"

CAIRNGORMS   1068M

DATE:	DISTANCE:	
WEATHER:	PEE	POO
TIME TAKEN:	ENJOYABLE ☆☆☆	

NOTES/PHOTOGRAPH/KEEP SAKE:

_____
_____
_____
_____
_____
_____
_____
_____
_____
_____
_____
_____
_____
_____

LOCHNAGAR

"THE LITTLE LOCH OF THE NOISY SOUND"

CAIRNGORMS	1155M

DATE:	DISTANCE:	
WEATHER:	PEE	POO
TIME TAKEN:	ENJOYABLE ☆☆☆	

NOTES/PHOTOGRAPH/KEEP SAKE:

_____
_____
_____
_____
_____
_____
_____
_____
_____
_____
_____
_____
_____

MEALL CHUAICH

"THE HILL OF THE QUAICH"

CAIRNGORMS   951M

DATE:	DISTANCE:	
WEATHER:	PEE	POO
TIME TAKEN:	ENJOYABLE ☆☆☆	

NOTES/PHOTOGRAPH/KEEP SAKE:

_____

_____

_____

_____

_____

_____

_____

_____

_____

_____

_____

_____

_____

_____

MONADH MOR

"THE BIG HILL"

CAIRNGORMS	1113M

DATE:	DISTANCE:	
WEATHER:	**PEE**	**POO**
TIME TAKEN:	**ENJOYABLE** ☆☆☆	

NOTES/PHOTOGRAPH/KEEP SAKE:

_____
_____
_____
_____
_____
_____
_____
_____
_____
_____
_____
_____
_____

MULLACH CLACH A'BHLAIR

"THE SUMMIT OF THE STONY PLAIN"

CAIRNGORMS   1019M

DATE:	DISTANCE:	
WEATHER:	PEE	POO
TIME TAKEN:	ENJOYABLE ☆☆☆	

NOTES/PHOTOGRAPH/KEEP SAKE:

_____
_____
_____
_____
_____
_____
_____
_____
_____
_____
_____
_____
_____

SGAIRNEACH MHOR

"THE BIG SCREE"

CAIRNGORMS		991M

DATE:	DISTANCE:	
WEATHER:	PEE	POO
TIME TAKEN:	ENJOYABLE ☆☆☆	

NOTES/PHOTOGRAPH/KEEP SAKE:

_____
_____
_____
_____
_____
_____
_____
_____
_____
_____
_____
_____
_____

SGOR AN LOCHAIN UAINE

"THE ROCKY PEAK OF THE LITTLE GREEN LOCH"

CAIRNGORMS   1258M

DATE:	DISTANCE:	
WEATHER:	PEE	POO
TIME TAKEN:	**ENJOYABLE** ☆☆☆	

NOTES/PHOTOGRAPH/KEEP SAKE:

_____

_____

_____

_____

_____

_____

_____

_____

_____

_____

_____

_____

_____

SGOR GAOITH

"THE WINDY PEAK"

CAIRNGORMS   1118M

DATE:	DISTANCE:	
WEATHER:	PEE	POO
TIME TAKEN:	**ENJOYABLE** ☆ ☆ ☆	

NOTES/PHOTOGRAPH/KEEP SAKE:

_____

_____

_____

_____

_____

_____

_____

_____

_____

_____

_____

_____

_____

THE CAIRNWELL

"THE PEAK OF BAGS"

CAIRNGORMS	933M

DATE:	DISTANCE:		
WEATHER:		**PEE**	**POO**
TIME TAKEN:	**ENJOYABLE** ☆☆☆		

NOTES/PHOTOGRAPH/KEEP SAKE:

_____

_____

_____

_____

_____

_____

_____

_____

_____

_____

_____

_____

_____

THE DEVIL'S POINT

"FROM BOD AN DEAMHAIN
MEANING PENIS OF THE DEMON"

CAIRNGORMS   1004M

DATE:	DISTANCE:	
WEATHER:	PEE	POO
TIME TAKEN:	ENJOYABLE ☆☆☆	

NOTES/PHOTOGRAPH/KEEP SAKE:

_____

_____

_____

_____

_____

_____

_____

_____

_____

_____

_____

_____

_____

TOLMOUNT
"THE VALLEY HILL"

CAIRNGORMS		958M	
DATE:	**DISTANCE:**		
WEATHER:		PEE	POO
TIME TAKEN:	**ENJOYABLE** ☆☆☆		

NOTES/PHOTOGRAPH/KEEP SAKE:

_____

_____

_____

_____

_____

_____

_____

_____

_____

_____

_____

_____

_____

_____

TOM BUIDHE
"THE YELLOW HILL"

CAIRNGORMS		957M

DATE:	DISTANCE:	
WEATHER:	PEE	POO
TIME TAKEN:	ENJOYABLE ☆☆☆	

NOTES/PHOTOGRAPH/KEEP SAKE:

_____
_____
_____
_____
_____
_____
_____
_____
_____
_____
_____
_____

AM BODACH
"THE OLD MAN"

FORT WILLIAM		1032M	
DATE:	**DISTANCE:**		
WEATHER:		**PEE**	**POO**
TIME TAKEN:	**ENJOYABLE** ☆☆☆		

NOTES/PHOTOGRAPH/KEEP SAKE:

_____
_____
_____
_____
_____
_____
_____
_____
_____
_____
_____
_____
_____

AN GEARANACH
"THE COMPLAINER"

FORT WILLIAM	982M

DATE:	DISTANCE:	
WEATHER:	PEE	POO
TIME TAKEN:	ENJOYABLE ☆☆☆	

NOTES/PHOTOGRAPH/KEEP SAKE:

_____
_____
_____
_____
_____
_____
_____
_____
_____
_____
_____
_____

AONACH BEAG (NEVIS RANGE)

"THE SMALL RIDGE"

FORT WILLIAM   1234M

DATE:	DISTANCE:	
WEATHER:	PEE	POO
TIME TAKEN:	ENJOYABLE ☆☆☆	

NOTES/PHOTOGRAPH/KEEP SAKE:

_____
_____
_____
_____
_____
_____
_____
_____
_____
_____
_____
_____
_____

AONACH MOR
"THE BIG RIDGE"

FORT WILLIAM		1221M

DATE:	DISTANCE:	
WEATHER:	PEE	POO
TIME TAKEN:	ENJOYABLE ☆☆☆	

NOTES/PHOTOGRAPH/KEEP SAKE:

_____
_____
_____
_____
_____
_____
_____
_____
_____
_____
_____
_____
_____
_____

BEINN A'CHAORAINN (GLEN SPEAN)

"THE HILL OF ROWAN"

FORT WILLIAM   1050M

DATE:	DISTANCE:		
WEATHER:		PEE	POO
TIME TAKEN:	ENJOYABLE ☆☆☆		

NOTES/PHOTOGRAPH/KEEP SAKE:

_____

_____

_____

_____

_____

_____

_____

_____

_____

_____

_____

_____

_____

BEINN A'CHLACHAIR

"THE HILL OF THE STONEMASON"

FORT WILLIAM   1087M

DATE:	DISTANCE:	
WEATHER:	PEE	POO
TIME TAKEN:	ENJOYABLE ☆☆☆	

NOTES/PHOTOGRAPH/KEEP SAKE:
_____
_____
_____
_____
_____
_____
_____
_____
_____
_____
_____
_____
_____

BEINN NA LAP

"THE DAPPLED HILL"

FORT WILLIAM 937M

DATE:	DISTANCE:	
WEATHER:	PEE	POO
TIME TAKEN:	ENJOYABLE ☆☆☆	

NOTES/PHOTOGRAPH/KEEP SAKE:

_____
_____
_____
_____
_____
_____
_____
_____
_____
_____
_____
_____
_____
_____

BEINN NAN AIGHENAN

"THE HILL OF THE HINDS"

FORT WILLIAM	960M

DATE:	DISTANCE:	
WEATHER:	PEE	POO
TIME TAKEN:	ENJOYABLE ☆☆☆	

NOTES/PHOTOGRAPH/KEEP SAKE:

_____
_____
_____
_____
_____
_____
_____
_____
_____
_____
_____
_____
_____

BEINN TEALLACH
"THE FORGE HILL"

FORT WILLIAM   915M

DATE:	DISTANCE:	
WEATHER:	PEE	POO
TIME TAKEN:	**ENJOYABLE** ☆☆☆	

NOTES/PHOTOGRAPH/KEEP SAKE:

_____
_____
_____
_____
_____
_____
_____
_____
_____
_____
_____
_____
_____

BEN NEVIS

"THE VENOMOUS MOUNTAIN"

FORT WILLIAM	1345M

DATE:	DISTANCE:	
WEATHER:	PEE	POO
TIME TAKEN:	ENJOYABLE ☆☆☆	

NOTES/PHOTOGRAPH/KEEP SAKE:

_____
_____
_____
_____
_____
_____
_____
_____
_____
_____
_____
_____
_____
_____

BEN STARAV
"THE HILL OF RUSTLING"

FORT WILLIAM	1078M

DATE:	DISTANCE:	
WEATHER:	PEE	POO
TIME TAKEN:	**ENJOYABLE** ☆☆☆	

NOTES/PHOTOGRAPH/KEEP SAKE:

_____
_____
_____
_____
_____
_____
_____
_____
_____
_____
_____
_____
_____
_____

BIDEAN NAM BIAN

"THE PINNACLE OF THE HILLS"

FORT WILLIAM   1150M

DATE:	DISTANCE:	
WEATHER:	PEE	POO
TIME TAKEN:	ENJOYABLE ☆☆☆	

NOTES/PHOTOGRAPH/KEEP SAKE:

_____
_____
_____
_____
_____
_____
_____
_____
_____
_____
_____
_____
_____

BINNEIN BEAG

"THE SMALL HILL"

FORT WILLIAM   943M

DATE:	DISTANCE:	
WEATHER:	PEE	POO
TIME TAKEN:	ENJOYABLE ☆☆☆	

NOTES/PHOTOGRAPH/KEEP SAKE:

_____

_____

_____

_____

_____

_____

_____

_____

_____

_____

_____

_____

_____

BINNEIN MOR

"THE LARGE PEAK"

FORT WILLIAM	1130M

DATE:	DISTANCE:	
WEATHER:	PEE	POO
TIME TAKEN:	ENJOYABLE ☆☆☆	

NOTES/PHOTOGRAPH/KEEP SAKE:

_____
_____
_____
_____
_____
_____
_____
_____
_____
_____
_____
_____

CARN DEARG (CORROUR)

"THE RED CAIRN LIKE PEAK"

FORT WILLIAM   941M

DATE:	DISTANCE:	
WEATHER:	PEE	POO
TIME TAKEN:	ENJOYABLE ☆☆☆	

NOTES/PHOTOGRAPH/KEEP SAKE:

_____
_____
_____
_____
_____
_____
_____
_____
_____
_____
_____
_____
_____
_____

CARN LIATH (CREAG MEAGAIDH)
"THE GREY PEAK"

FORT WILLIAM	1006M	

DATE:	DISTANCE:	
WEATHER:	PEE	POO
TIME TAKEN:	ENJOYABLE ☆☆☆	

NOTES/PHOTOGRAPH/KEEP SAKE:

_____
_____
_____
_____
_____
_____
_____
_____
_____
_____
_____
_____
_____
_____

CARN MOR DEARG

"THE LARGE RED CAIRN LIKE PEAK"

FORT WILLIAM	1220M

DATE:	DISTANCE:	
WEATHER:	**PEE**	**POO**
TIME TAKEN:	**ENJOYABLE** ☆☆☆	

NOTES/PHOTOGRAPH/KEEP SAKE:

_____

_____

_____

_____

_____

_____

_____

_____

_____

_____

_____

_____

_____

CHNO DEARG
"THE RED HILL"

FORT WILLIAM   1046M

DATE:	DISTANCE:	
WEATHER:	PEE	POO
TIME TAKEN:	**ENJOYABLE** ☆ ☆ ☆	

NOTES/PHOTOGRAPH/KEEP SAKE:

_____
_____
_____
_____
_____
_____
_____
_____
_____
_____
_____
_____
_____

CREAG MEAGAIDH

"THE BOGLAND CRAG"

FORT WILLIAM   1130M

DATE:	DISTANCE:	
WEATHER:	PEE	POO
TIME TAKEN:	ENJOYABLE ☆☆☆	

NOTES/PHOTOGRAPH/KEEP SAKE:

_____
_____
_____
_____
_____
_____
_____
_____
_____
_____
_____
_____
_____
_____

CREAG PITRIDH

"THE PETRIE'S CRAG"

FORT WILLIAM   924M

DATE:	DISTANCE:	
WEATHER:	PEE	POO
TIME TAKEN:	ENJOYABLE ☆☆☆	

NOTES/PHOTOGRAPH/KEEP SAKE:

_____
_____
_____
_____
_____
_____
_____
_____
_____
_____
_____
_____
_____
_____

CREISE

"THE GREASE OR FAT"

FORT WILLIAM	1100M

DATE:	DISTANCE:	
WEATHER:	PEE	POO
TIME TAKEN:	ENJOYABLE ☆☆☆	

NOTES/PHOTOGRAPH/KEEP SAKE:

_____

_____

_____

_____

_____

_____

_____

_____

_____

_____

_____

_____

_____

_____

GAIRICH
"THE NOISY HILL"

FORT WILLIAM   919M

DATE:	DISTANCE:		
WEATHER:		PEE	POO
TIME TAKEN:	ENJOYABLE ☆☆☆		

NOTES/PHOTOGRAPH/KEEP SAKE:
_____
_____
_____
_____
_____
_____
_____
_____
_____
_____
_____
_____

GARBH CHIOCH MHOR
"THE BIG ROUGH BREAST"

FORT WILLIAM   1013M

DATE:	DISTANCE:	
WEATHER:	PEE	POO
TIME TAKEN:	ENJOYABLE ☆☆☆	

NOTES/PHOTOGRAPH/KEEP SAKE:

_____

_____

_____

_____

_____

_____

_____

_____

_____

_____

_____

_____

_____

GEAL CHARN
"THE WHITE PEAK"

FORT WILLIAM		1049M

DATE:	DISTANCE:	
WEATHER:	PEE	POO
TIME TAKEN:	ENJOYABLE ☆☆☆	

NOTES/PHOTOGRAPH/KEEP SAKE:

_____
_____
_____
_____
_____
_____
_____
_____
_____
_____
_____
_____
_____
_____

GLAS BHEINN MHOR

"THE BIG GREEN HILL"

FORT WILLIAM   997M

DATE:	DISTANCE:	
WEATHER:	PEE	POO
TIME TAKEN:	ENJOYABLE ☆☆☆	

NOTES/PHOTOGRAPH/KEEP SAKE:

_____

_____

_____

_____

_____

_____

_____

_____

_____

_____

_____

_____

_____

_____

GLEOURAICH

"THE NOISY HILL"

FORT WILLIAM   1035M

DATE:	DISTANCE:	
WEATHER:	PEE	POO
TIME TAKEN:	**ENJOYABLE** ☆☆☆	

NOTES/PHOTOGRAPH/KEEP SAKE:

_____

_____

_____

_____

_____

_____

_____

_____

_____

_____

_____

_____

GULVAIN

"THE DIRTY HILL"

FORT WILLIAM   987M

DATE:	DISTANCE:	
WEATHER:	PEE	POO
TIME TAKEN:	**ENJOYABLE** ☆☆☆	

NOTES/PHOTOGRAPH/KEEP SAKE:

_____
_____
_____
_____
_____
_____
_____
_____
_____
_____
_____
_____
_____
_____
_____

LADHAR BHEINN

"THE HILL OF THE HOOF"

FORT WILLIAM   1020M

DATE:	DISTANCE:	
WEATHER:	**PEE**	**POO**
TIME TAKEN:	**ENJOYABLE** ☆☆☆	

NOTES/PHOTOGRAPH/KEEP SAKE:

_____

_____

_____

_____

_____

_____

_____

_____

_____

_____

_____

_____

_____

LUINNE BHEINN

"THE ANGRY HILL"

FORT WILLIAM   939M

DATE:	DISTANCE:	
WEATHER:	PEE	POO
TIME TAKEN:	ENJOYABLE ☆☆☆	

NOTES/PHOTOGRAPH/KEEP SAKE:

_____
_____
_____
_____
_____
_____
_____
_____
_____
_____
_____
_____
_____
_____

MEALL A'BHUIRIDH

"THE HILL OF THE BELLOWING"

FORT WILLIAM   1108M

DATE:	DISTANCE:	
WEATHER:	PEE	POO
TIME TAKEN:	ENJOYABLE ☆☆☆	

NOTES/PHOTOGRAPH/KEEP SAKE:

_____
_____
_____
_____
_____
_____
_____
_____
_____
_____
_____
_____
_____
_____

MEALL BUIDHE (KNOYDART)

"THE YELLOW HILL"

FORT WILLIAM   946M

DATE:	DISTANCE:	
WEATHER:	**PEE**	**POO**
TIME TAKEN:	**ENJOYABLE** ☆☆☆	

NOTES/PHOTOGRAPH/KEEP SAKE:

_____
_____
_____
_____
_____
_____
_____
_____
_____
_____
_____
_____
_____
_____

MEALL DEARG (AONACH EAGACH)
"THE RED HILL"

FORT WILLIAM	953M

DATE:	DISTANCE:	
WEATHER:	PEE	POO
TIME TAKEN:	ENJOYABLE ☆☆☆	

NOTES/PHOTOGRAPH/KEEP SAKE:

_____

_____

_____

_____

_____

_____

_____

_____

_____

_____

_____

_____

_____

_____

_____

MEALL NA TEANGA

"THE ROUNDED HILL OF THE TONGUE"

FORT WILLIAM	918M

DATE:	DISTANCE:	
WEATHER:	PEE	POO
TIME TAKEN:	ENJOYABLE ☆☆☆	

NOTES/PHOTOGRAPH/KEEP SAKE:
_____
_____
_____
_____
_____
_____
_____
_____
_____
_____
_____
_____
_____

MEALL NAN EUN

"THE HILL OF THE BIRD"

FORT WILLIAM   928M

DATE:	DISTANCE:	
WEATHER:	PEE	POO
TIME TAKEN:	ENJOYABLE ☆☆☆	

NOTES/PHOTOGRAPH/KEEP SAKE:

_____

_____

_____

_____

_____

_____

_____

_____

_____

_____

_____

_____

MULLACH NAN COIREAN

"THE SUMMIT OF THE CORRIES"

FORT WILLIAM	939M

DATE:	DISTANCE:	
WEATHER:	PEE	POO
TIME TAKEN:	**ENJOYABLE** ☆☆☆	

NOTES/PHOTOGRAPH/KEEP SAKE:

_____

_____

_____

_____

_____

_____

_____

_____

_____

_____

_____

_____

_____

_____

NA GRUAGAICHEAN

"THE MAIDENS"

FORT WILLIAM	1056M

DATE:	DISTANCE:	
WEATHER:	PEE	POO
TIME TAKEN:	**ENJOYABLE** ☆☆☆	

NOTES/PHOTOGRAPH/KEEP SAKE:

_____
_____
_____
_____
_____
_____
_____
_____
_____
_____
_____
_____
_____
_____

SGOR GAIBHRE

"THE ROCKY PEAK OF THE GOAT"

FORT WILLIAM   955M

DATE:	DISTANCE:	
WEATHER:	**PEE**	**POO**
TIME TAKEN:	**ENJOYABLE** ☆☆☆	

NOTES/PHOTOGRAPH/KEEP SAKE:

_____
_____
_____
_____
_____
_____
_____
_____
_____
_____
_____
_____
_____
_____

SGOR NA H-ULAIDH

"THE ROCKY PEAK OF TREASURE"

FORT WILLIAM   994M

DATE:	DISTANCE:	
WEATHER:	PEE	POO
TIME TAKEN:	ENJOYABLE ☆☆☆	

NOTES/PHOTOGRAPH/KEEP SAKE:

_____
_____
_____
_____
_____
_____
_____
_____
_____
_____
_____
_____
_____
_____

SGORR DHEARG (BEINN A'BHEITHIR)

"THE RED ROCKY PEAK"

FORT WILLIAM   1024M

DATE:	DISTANCE:	
WEATHER:	PEE	POO
TIME TAKEN:	ENNJOYABLE ☆☆☆	

NOTES/PHOTOGRAPH/KEEP SAKE:

_____
_____
_____
_____
_____
_____
_____
_____
_____
_____
_____
_____
_____

SGORR DHONUILL (BEINN A'BHEITHIR)

"THE DONALD'S ROCKY PEAK"

FORT WILLIAM	1001M

DATE:	DISTANCE:	
WEATHER:	PEE	POO
TIME TAKEN:	ENJOYABLE ☆ ☆ ☆	

NOTES/PHOTOGRAPH/KEEP SAKE:

_____
_____
_____
_____
_____
_____
_____
_____
_____
_____
_____
_____
_____

SGORR NAM FIANNAIDH (AONACH EAGACH)

"THE ROCKY PEAK OF FIAN WARRIORS"

FORT WILLIAM	967M

DATE:	DISTANCE:	
WEATHER:	PEE	POO
TIME TAKEN:	ENJOYABLE ☆☆☆	

NOTES/PHOTOGRAPH/KEEP SAKE:

_____

_____

_____

_____

_____

_____

_____

_____

_____

_____

_____

_____

_____

SGURR A'MHAIM

*"THE ROCKY PEAK OF THE LARGE
ROUNDED HILL"*

FORT WILLIAM   1099M

DATE:	DISTANCE:	
WEATHER:	PEE	POO
TIME TAKEN:	**ENJOYABLE** ☆☆☆	

NOTES/PHOTOGRAPH/KEEP SAKE:

_____
_____
_____
_____
_____
_____
_____
_____
_____
_____
_____
_____
_____

SGURR A'MHAORAICH

"THE ROCKY PEAK OF THE SHELLFISH"

FORT WILLIAM   1027M

DATE:	DISTANCE:	
WEATHER:	PEE	POO
TIME TAKEN:	ENJOYABLE ☆☆☆	

NOTES/PHOTOGRAPH/KEEP SAKE:

_____
_____
_____
_____
_____
_____
_____
_____
_____
_____
_____
_____
_____

SGURR CHOINNICH MOR

"THE BIG ROCKY PEAK OF THE MOSS"

FORT WILLIAM		1094M

DATE:	DISTANCE:	
WEATHER:	PEE	POO
TIME TAKEN:	ENJOYABLE ☆☆☆	

NOTES/PHOTOGRAPH/KEEP SAKE:

_____

_____

_____

_____

_____

_____

_____

_____

_____

_____

_____

_____

_____

_____

SGURR EILDE MOR

"THE LARGE ROCKY PEAK OF THE HIND"

FORT WILLIAM   **1010M**

DATE:	DISTANCE:	
WEATHER:	**PEE**	**POO**
TIME TAKEN:	**ENJOYABLE** ☆☆☆	

NOTES/PHOTOGRAPH/KEEP SAKE:

_____
_____
_____
_____
_____
_____
_____
_____
_____
_____
_____
_____
_____
_____

SGURR MOR (LOCH QUOICH)

"THE BIG ROCKY PEAK"

FORT WILLIAM   1003M

DATE:	DISTANCE:	
WEATHER:	PEE	POO
TIME TAKEN:	ENJOYABLE ☆☆☆	

NOTES/PHOTOGRAPH/KEEP SAKE:

_____

_____

_____

_____

_____

_____

_____

_____

_____

_____

_____

_____

_____

SGURR NA CICHE

"THE ROCKY PEAK OF THE BREAST"

FORT WILLIAM   1040M

DATE:	DISTANCE:	
WEATHER:	**PEE**	**POO**
TIME TAKEN:	**ENJOYABLE** ☆☆☆	

NOTES/PHOTOGRAPH/KEEP SAKE:

_____

_____

_____

_____

_____

_____

_____

_____

_____

_____

_____

_____

_____

SGURR NAN COIREACHAN (GLEN DESSARY)

"THE ROCKY PEAK OF THE CORRIES"

FORT WILLIAM   953M

DATE:	DISTANCE:	
WEATHER:	PEE	POO
TIME TAKEN:	ENJOYABLE ☆☆☆	

NOTES/PHOTOGRAPH/KEEP SAKE:

_____
_____
_____
_____
_____
_____
_____
_____
_____
_____
_____
_____
_____
_____

SGURR NAN COIREACHAN (GLENFINNAN)

"THE ROCKY PEAK OF THE CORRIES"

FORT WILLIAM   956M

DATE:	DISTANCE:	
WEATHER:	PEE	POO
TIME TAKEN:	ENJOYABLE ☆☆☆	

NOTES/PHOTOGRAPH/KEEP SAKE:

_____
_____
_____
_____
_____
_____
_____
_____
_____
_____
_____
_____
_____

SGURR THUILM

"THE ROCKY PEAK OF THE HILLOCK"

FORT WILLIAM   963M

DATE:	DISTANCE:		
WEATHER:	PEE		POO
TIME TAKEN:	ENJOYABLE ☆☆☆		

NOTES/PHOTOGRAPH/KEEP SAKE:

_____
_____
_____
_____
_____
_____
_____
_____
_____
_____
_____
_____
_____
_____

SPIDEAN MIALACH
"THE PEAK OF DEER"

FORT WILLIAM   996M

DATE:	DISTANCE:	
WEATHER:	PEE	POO
TIME TAKEN:	ENJOYABLE ☆☆☆	

NOTES/PHOTOGRAPH/KEEP SAKE:

_____
_____
_____
_____
_____
_____
_____
_____
_____
_____
_____
_____
_____

SRON A'CHOIRE GHAIRBH

"THE PEAK OF THE ROUGH CORRIE"

FORT WILLIAM	937M

DATE:	DISTANCE:	
WEATHER:	PEE	POO
TIME TAKEN:	**ENJOYABLE** ☆ ☆ ☆	

NOTES/PHOTOGRAPH/KEEP SAKE:

_____
_____
_____
_____
_____
_____
_____
_____
_____
_____
_____
_____
_____

STOB A'CHOIRE MHEADHOIN

"THE PEAK OF THE MIDDLE CORRIE"

FORT WILLIAM   1106M

DATE:	DISTANCE:	
WEATHER:	PEE	POO
TIME TAKEN:	ENJOYABLE ☆☆☆	

NOTES/PHOTOGRAPH/KEEP SAKE:

_____

_____

_____

_____

_____

_____

_____

_____

_____

_____

_____

_____

_____

_____

STOB BAN (GREY CORRIES)

"THE WHITE PEAK"

FORT WILLIAM	977M

DATE:	DISTANCE:	
WEATHER:	PEE	POO
TIME TAKEN:	ENJOYABLE ☆☆☆	

NOTES/PHOTOGRAPH/KEEP SAKE:

_____
_____
_____
_____
_____
_____
_____
_____
_____
_____
_____
_____
_____
_____
_____

STOB BAN (MAMORES)

"THE WHITE PEAK"

FORT WILLIAM   999M

DATE:	DISTANCE:	
WEATHER:	PEE	POO
TIME TAKEN:	\[ENJOYABLE\] ☆☆☆	

NOTES/PHOTOGRAPH/KEEP SAKE:

_____

_____

_____

_____

_____

_____

_____

_____

_____

_____

_____

_____

_____

_____

STOB CHOIRE CLAURIGH

"THE PEAK OF CORRIE OF BRAWLING OR BELLOWING"

FORT WILLIAM   1177M

DATE:	DISTANCE:	
WEATHER:	PEE	POO
TIME TAKEN:	ENJOYABLE ☆☆☆	

NOTES/PHOTOGRAPH/KEEP SAKE:

_____
_____
_____
_____
_____
_____
_____
_____
_____
_____
_____
_____
_____
_____

STOB COIR AN ALBANNAICH

"THE PEAK OF THE SCOTSMAN'S CORRIE"

FORT WILLIAM   1044M

DATE:	DISTANCE:	
WEATHER:	PEE	POO
TIME TAKEN:	ENJOYABLE ☆☆☆	

NOTES/PHOTOGRAPH/KEEP SAKE:

_____

_____

_____

_____

_____

_____

_____

_____

_____

_____

_____

_____

_____

STOB COIRE A'CHAIRN

"THE PEAK OF THE CORRIE OF THE CAIRN"

FORT WILLIAM   981M

DATE:	DISTANCE:	
WEATHER:	PEE	POO
TIME TAKEN:	**ENJOYABLE** ☆☆☆	

NOTES/PHOTOGRAPH/KEEP SAKE:

_____
_____
_____
_____
_____
_____
_____
_____
_____
_____
_____
_____
_____

STOB COIRE AN LAOIGH

"THE PEAK OF THE CORRIE OF THE CALF"

FORT WILLIAM   1116M

DATE:	DISTANCE:	
WEATHER:	PEE	POO
TIME TAKEN:	ENJOYABLE ☆☆☆	

NOTES/PHOTOGRAPH/KEEP SAKE:

_____

_____

_____

_____

_____

_____

_____

_____

_____

_____

_____

_____

_____

STOB COIRE EASAIN

*"THE PEAK OF THE CORRIE OF THE
LITTLE WATERFALL"*

FORT WILLIAM   1115M

DATE:	DISTANCE:	
WEATHER:	PEE	POO
TIME TAKEN:	ENJOYABLE ☆☆☆	

NOTES/PHOTOGRAPH/KEEP SAKE:

_____
_____
_____
_____
_____
_____
_____
_____
_____
_____
_____
_____
_____
_____
_____

STOB COIRE RAINEACH (BUACHAILLE ETIVE BEAG)

"THE PEAK OF THE BRACKEN FILLED CORRIE"

FORT WILLIAM   925M

DATE:	DISTANCE:	
WEATHER:	PEE	POO
TIME TAKEN:	ENJOYABLE ☆☆☆	

NOTES/PHOTOGRAPH/KEEP SAKE:

_____
_____
_____
_____
_____
_____
_____
_____
_____
_____
_____
_____
_____
_____

STOB COIRE SGREAMHACH

"THE PEAK OF THE DREADFUL CORRIE"

FORT WILLIAM   1072M

DATE:	DISTANCE:	
WEATHER:	PEE	POO
TIME TAKEN:	ENJOYABLE ☆ ☆ ☆	

NOTES/PHOTOGRAPH/KEEP SAKE:

_____
_____
_____
_____
_____
_____
_____
_____
_____
_____
_____
_____
_____

STOB COIRE SGRIODAIN

"THE PEAK OF THE SCREE CORRIE"

FORT WILLIAM   979M

DATE:	DISTANCE:

WEATHER:	PEE	POO

TIME TAKEN:	ENJOYABLE ☆☆☆

NOTES/PHOTOGRAPH/KEEP SAKE:

_____
_____
_____
_____
_____
_____
_____
_____
_____
_____
_____
_____
_____
_____

STOB DEARG (BUACHAILLE ETIVE MOR)
"THE RED PEAK"

FORT WILLIAM   1021M

DATE:	DISTANCE:	
WEATHER:	PEE	POO
TIME TAKEN:	ENJOYABLE ☆☆☆	

NOTES/PHOTOGRAPH/KEEP SAKE:

_____

_____

_____

_____

_____

_____

_____

_____

_____

_____

_____

_____

_____

_____

STOB DUBH (BUACHAILLE ETIVE BEAG)

"THE BLACK PEAK"

FORT WILLIAM   956M

DATE:	DISTANCE:		
WEATHER:		PEE	POO
TIME TAKEN:	ENJOYABLE ☆☆☆		

NOTES/PHOTOGRAPH/KEEP SAKE:

_____
_____
_____
_____
_____
_____
_____
_____
_____
_____
_____
_____
_____
_____

STOB NA BROIGE (BUACHAILLE ETIVE MOR)

"THE PEAK OF THE SHOE"

FORT WILLIAM	956M

DATE:	DISTANCE:	
WEATHER:	PEE	POO
TIME TAKEN:	ENJOYABLE ☆☆☆	

NOTES/PHOTOGRAPH/KEEP SAKE:

_____
_____
_____
_____
_____
_____
_____
_____
_____
_____
_____
_____
_____

STOB POITE COIRE ARDAIR

"THE POINTED HILL OF THE POT OF THE HIGH CORRIE"

FORT WILLIAM   1054M

DATE:	DISTANCE:	
WEATHER:	PEE	POO
TIME TAKEN:	ENJOYABLE ☆☆☆	

NOTES/PHOTOGRAPH/KEEP SAKE:

_____
_____
_____
_____
_____
_____
_____
_____
_____
_____
_____
_____
_____

AM BASTEIR
"THE EXECUTIONER"

ISLANDS		934M	
DATE:	DISTANCE:		
WEATHER:		PEE	POO
TIME TAKEN:	ENJOYABLE ☆☆☆		

NOTES/PHOTOGRAPH/KEEP SAKE:

_____
_____
_____
_____
_____
_____
_____
_____
_____
_____
_____
_____
_____
_____

BEN MORE (MULL)

"THE BIG MOUNTAIN"

ISLANDS	966M

DATE:	DISTANCE:	

WEATHER:	PEE	POO

TIME TAKEN:	ENJOYABLE ☆☆☆

NOTES/PHOTOGRAPH/KEEP SAKE:

_____

_____

_____

_____

_____

_____

_____

_____

_____

_____

_____

_____

_____

BLA BHEINN

"THE BLUE MOUNTAIN"

ISLANDS		928M	
DATE:	**DISTANCE:**		
WEATHER:		PEE	POO
TIME TAKEN:	ENJOYABLE ☆☆☆		

NOTES/PHOTOGRAPH/KEEP SAKE:

_____
_____
_____
_____
_____
_____
_____
_____
_____
_____
_____
_____
_____
_____

BRUACH NA FRITHE

"THE SLOPE OF THE DEER FOREST"

ISLANDS	958M

DATE:	DISTANCE:	
WEATHER:	PEE	POO
TIME TAKEN:	**ENJOYABLE** ☆☆☆	

NOTES/PHOTOGRAPH/KEEP SAKE:

_____

_____

_____

_____

_____

_____

_____

_____

_____

_____

_____

_____

SGURR DEARG(INACCESSIBLE PINNACLE)

"THE RED ROCKY PEAK"

ISLANDS	986M

DATE:	DISTANCE:	

WEATHER:	PEE	POO

TIME TAKEN:	ENJOYABLE ☆ ☆ ☆

NOTES/PHOTOGRAPH/KEEP SAKE:

_____

_____

_____

_____

_____

_____

_____

_____

_____

_____

_____

_____

_____

_____

SGURR A'GHREADAIDH

"THE ROCKY PEAK OF TORMENT"

ISLANDS		973M	
DATE:	DISTANCE:		
WEATHER:	PEE		POO
TIME TAKEN:	ENJOYABLE ☆☆☆		

NOTES/PHOTOGRAPH/KEEP SAKE:

_____
_____
_____
_____
_____
_____
_____
_____
_____
_____
_____
_____
_____

SGURR A'MHADAIDH

"THE ROCKY PEAK OF THE FOX"

ISLANDS		918M

DATE:	DISTANCE:	
WEATHER:	PEE	POO
TIME TAKEN:	ENJOYABLE ☆☆☆	

NOTES/PHOTOGRAPH/KEEP SAKE:

_____
_____
_____
_____
_____
_____
_____
_____
_____
_____
_____
_____

SGURR ALASDAIR

"THE ALASDAIR'S ROCKY PEAK"

ISLANDS	992M

DATE:	DISTANCE:	
WEATHER:	PEE	POO
TIME TAKEN:	ENJOYABLE ☆☆☆	

NOTES/PHOTOGRAPH/KEEP SAKE:

_____

_____

_____

_____

_____

_____

_____

_____

_____

_____

_____

_____

SGURR DUBH MOR

"THE BIG BLACK ROCKY PEAK"

ISLANDS	944M

DATE:	DISTANCE:	
WEATHER:	PEE	POO
TIME TAKEN:	ENJOYABLE ☆☆☆	

NOTES/PHOTOGRAPH/KEEP SAKE:

_____
_____
_____
_____
_____
_____
_____
_____
_____
_____
_____
_____
_____

SGURR MHIC CHOINNICH

"THE MACKENZIE'S ROCKY PEAK"

ISLANDS	948M

DATE:	DISTANCE:	
WEATHER:	PEE	POO
TIME TAKEN:	ENJOYABLE ☆☆☆	

NOTES/PHOTOGRAPH/KEEP SAKE:

_____
_____
_____
_____
_____
_____
_____
_____
_____
_____
_____
_____
_____

SGURR NA BANACHDICH

"THE ROCKY PEAK OF THE MILKMAID"

ISLANDS		965M	
DATE:	**DISTANCE:**		
WEATHER:		**PEE**	**POO**
TIME TAKEN:	**ENJOYABLE** ☆☆☆		

NOTES/PHOTOGRAPH/KEEP SAKE:

_____

_____

_____

_____

_____

_____

_____

_____

_____

_____

_____

_____

_____

_____

SGURR NAN EAG

"THE ROCKY PEAK OF THE NOTCHES"

ISLANDS	924M

DATE:	DISTANCE:	
WEATHER:	PEE	POO
TIME TAKEN:	ENJOYABLE ☆☆☆	

NOTES/PHOTOGRAPH/KEEP SAKE:

_____
_____
_____
_____
_____
_____
_____
_____
_____
_____
_____
_____
_____

SGURR NAN GILLEAN

"THE ROCKY PEAK OF THE YOUNG MEN"

ISLANDS   964M

DATE:	DISTANCE:	
WEATHER:	PEE	POO
TIME TAKEN:	ENJOYABLE ☆☆☆	

NOTES/PHOTOGRAPH/KEEP SAKE:

_____
_____
_____
_____
_____
_____
_____
_____
_____
_____
_____
_____
_____
_____

A' CHRALAIG
"THE BASKET"

KINTAIL   1120M

DATE:	DISTANCE:		
WEATHER:		PEE	POO
TIME TAKEN:	ENJOYABLE ☆☆☆		

NOTES/PHOTOGRAPH/KEEP SAKE:

_____
_____
_____
_____
_____
_____
_____
_____
_____
_____
_____
_____
_____
_____

A' GHLAS-BHEINN

"THE GREY HILL"

KINTAIL   918M

DATE:	DISTANCE:	
WEATHER:	PEE	POO
TIME TAKEN:	ENJOYABLE ☆☆☆	

NOTES/PHOTOGRAPH/KEEP SAKE:

_____
_____
_____
_____
_____
_____
_____
_____
_____
_____
_____
_____
_____

AONACH AIR CHRITH

"THE TREMBLING RIDGE"

KINTAIL   1021M

DATE:	DISTANCE:	
WEATHER:	PEE	POO
TIME TAKEN:	ENJOYABLE ☆☆☆	

NOTES/PHOTOGRAPH/KEEP SAKE:

_____
_____
_____
_____
_____
_____
_____
_____
_____
_____
_____
_____
_____

AONACH MEADHOIN

"THE MIDDLE RIDGE"

KINTAIL	1001M

DATE:	DISTANCE:

WEATHER:	PEE	POO

TIME TAKEN:	ENJOYABLE ☆ ☆ ☆

NOTES/PHOTOGRAPH/KEEP SAKE:

_____

_____

_____

_____

_____

_____

_____

_____

_____

_____

_____

_____

_____

BEINN FHADA

"THE LONG MOUNTAIN"

KINTAIL	1032M

DATE:	DISTANCE:	

WEATHER:	PEE	POO

TIME TAKEN:	ENJOYABLE ☆☆☆

NOTES/PHOTOGRAPH/KEEP SAKE:

_____

_____

_____

_____

_____

_____

_____

_____

_____

_____

_____

_____

_____

BEINN SGRITHEALL

"THE SCREE HILL"

KINTAIL   974M

DATE:	DISTANCE:	
WEATHER:	PEE	POO
TIME TAKEN:	ENJOYABLE ☆☆☆	

NOTES/PHOTOGRAPH/KEEP SAKE:

_____
_____
_____
_____
_____
_____
_____
_____
_____
_____
_____
_____
_____
_____

CARN GHLUASAID

"THE CAIRN LIKE HILL OF MOVEMENT"

KINTAIL	957M

DATE:	DISTANCE:	

WEATHER:	PEE	POO

TIME TAKEN:	ENJOYABLE ☆☆☆

NOTES/PHOTOGRAPH/KEEP SAKE:

_____
_____
_____
_____
_____
_____
_____
_____
_____
_____
_____
_____
_____

CISTE DHUBH

"THE BLACK CHEST"

KINTAIL	979M

DATE:	DISTANCE:	
WEATHER:	PEE	POO
TIME TAKEN:	ENJOYABLE ☆☆☆	

NOTES/PHOTOGRAPH/KEEP SAKE:

_____
_____
_____
_____
_____
_____
_____
_____
_____
_____
_____
_____
_____

CREAG A'MHAIM

"THE CRAG OF THE LARGE ROUNDED HILL"

KINTAIL	947M

DATE:	DISTANCE:	
WEATHER:	PEE	POO
TIME TAKEN:	**ENJOYABLE** ☆☆☆	

NOTES/PHOTOGRAPH/KEEP SAKE:

_____
_____
_____
_____
_____
_____
_____
_____
_____
_____
_____
_____
_____
_____

CREAG NAN DAMH

"THE CRAG OF THE STAGS"

| KINTAIL | 918M |

DATE:	DISTANCE:	
WEATHER:	PEE	POO
TIME TAKEN:	ENJOYABLE ☆☆☆	

NOTES/PHOTOGRAPH/KEEP SAKE:

_____
_____
_____
_____
_____
_____
_____
_____
_____
_____
_____
_____
_____
_____

DRUIM SHIONNACH

"THE RIDGE OF FOXES"

KINTAIL   987M

DATE:	DISTANCE:		
WEATHER:		PEE	POO
TIME TAKEN:	ENJOYABLE ☆☆☆		

NOTES/PHOTOGRAPH/KEEP SAKE:

_____

_____

_____

_____

_____

_____

_____

_____

_____

_____

_____

_____

_____

MAOL CHINN-DEARG

"THE BALD RED HEAD"

KINTAIL		981M

DATE:	DISTANCE:	
WEATHER:	PEE	POO
TIME TAKEN:	ENJOYABLE ☆☆☆	

NOTES/PHOTOGRAPH/KEEP SAKE:

_____
_____
_____
_____
_____
_____
_____
_____
_____
_____
_____
_____
_____

MULLACH FRAOCH-CHOIRE

"THE SUMMIT OF THE HEATHERY CORRIE"

KINTAIL		1102M	
DATE:	**DISTANCE:**		
WEATHER:		**PEE**	**POO**
TIME TAKEN:	**ENJOYABLE** ☆☆☆		

NOTES/PHOTOGRAPH/KEEP SAKE:

_____
_____
_____
_____
_____
_____
_____
_____
_____
_____
_____
_____
_____

SAIL CHAORAINN

"THE ROUNDED HILL OF THE ROWAN TREE"

KINTAIL	1002M

DATE:	DISTANCE:	
WEATHER:	**PEE**	**POO**
TIME TAKEN:	**ENJOYABLE** ☆☆☆	

NOTES/PHOTOGRAPH/KEEP SAKE:

_____
_____
_____
_____
_____
_____
_____
_____
_____
_____
_____
_____
_____

SAILEAG

"THE LITTLE OR NOTCHED HEEL"

KINTAIL	956M

DATE:	DISTANCE:	
WEATHER:	**PEE**	**POO**
TIME TAKEN:	**ENJOYABLE** ☆☆☆	

NOTES/PHOTOGRAPH/KEEP SAKE:

_____
_____
_____
_____
_____
_____
_____
_____
_____
_____
_____
_____
_____

SGURR A'BHEALAICH DHEIRG

"THE ROCKY PEAK OF THE RED PASS"

KINTAIL	1036M

DATE:	DISTANCE:	
WEATHER:	PEE	POO
TIME TAKEN:	ENJOYABLE ☆ ☆ ☆	

NOTES/PHOTOGRAPH/KEEP SAKE:

_____

_____

_____

_____

_____

_____

_____

_____

_____

_____

_____

_____

_____

SGURR AN DOIRE LEATHAIN

"THE ROCKY PEAK OF BROAD OAK THICKET"

KINTAIL	1010M

DATE:	DISTANCE:		
WEATHER:	PEE		POO
TIME TAKEN:	ENJOYABLE ☆☆☆		

NOTES/PHOTOGRAPH/KEEP SAKE:

_____
_____
_____
_____
_____
_____
_____
_____
_____
_____
_____
_____
_____

SGURR AN LOCHAIN

"THE ROCKY PEAK OF THE LITTLE LOCH"

KINTAIL   1004M

DATE:	DISTANCE:	
WEATHER:	PEE	POO
TIME TAKEN:	ENJOYABLE ☆☆☆	

NOTES/PHOTOGRAPH/KEEP SAKE:

_____

_____

_____

_____

_____

_____

_____

_____

_____

_____

_____

_____

_____

SGURR FHUARAN

"THE ROCKY PEAK OF THE WOLF"

KINTAIL	1067M

DATE:	DISTANCE:		
WEATHER:		PEE	POO
TIME TAKEN:	ENJOYABLE ☆ ☆ ☆		

NOTES/PHOTOGRAPH/KEEP SAKE:

_____
_____
_____
_____
_____
_____
_____
_____
_____
_____
_____
_____
_____

SGURR NA CARNACH

"THE ROCKY PEAK OF THE CAIRNS"

KINTAIL	1002M

DATE:	DISTANCE:	
WEATHER:	PEE	POO
TIME TAKEN:	ENJOYABLE ☆☆☆	

NOTES/PHOTOGRAPH/KEEP SAKE:

_____
_____
_____
_____
_____
_____
_____
_____
_____
_____
_____
_____
_____

SGURR NA CISTE DUIBHE

"THE ROCKY PEAK OF THE BLACK CHEST"

KINTAIL   1027M

DATE:	DISTANCE:		
WEATHER:		PEE	POO
TIME TAKEN:	ENJOYABLE ☆☆☆		

NOTES/PHOTOGRAPH/KEEP SAKE:

_____
_____
_____
_____
_____
_____
_____
_____
_____
_____
_____
_____
_____

SGURR NA SGINE

"THE ROCKY PEAK OF THE KNIFE"

KINTAIL	945M

DATE:	DISTANCE:	
WEATHER:	PEE	POO
TIME TAKEN:	ENJOYABLE ☆☆☆	

NOTES/PHOTOGRAPH/KEEP SAKE:

_____
_____
_____
_____
_____
_____
_____
_____
_____
_____
_____
_____
_____

SGURR NAN CONBHAIREAN

"THE ROCKY PEAK OF THE HOUND KEEPER"

KINTAIL	1109M

DATE:	DISTANCE:	
WEATHER:	PEE	POO
TIME TAKEN:	ENJOYABLE ☆☆☆	

NOTES/PHOTOGRAPH/KEEP SAKE:

_____
_____
_____
_____
_____
_____
_____
_____
_____
_____
_____
_____
_____

THE SADDLE

KINTAIL		1010M	
DATE:	DISTANCE:		
WEATHER:	PEE	POO	
TIME TAKEN:	ENJOYABLE ☆☆☆		

NOTES/PHOTOGRAPH/KEEP SAKE:

_____
_____
_____
_____
_____
_____
_____
_____
_____
_____
_____
_____
_____
_____

AN CAISTEAL

"THE CASTLE"

LOCH LOMOND	995M

DATE:	DISTANCE:	
WEATHER:	PEE	POO

TIME TAKEN:	ENJOYABLE ☆☆☆

NOTES/PHOTOGRAPH/KEEP SAKE:

_____
_____
_____
_____
_____
_____
_____
_____
_____
_____
_____
_____
_____

BEINN A'CHROIN

"THE HILL OF THE SHEEPFOLD"

LOCH LOMOND		942M

DATE:	DISTANCE:	
WEATHER:	PEE	POO
TIME TAKEN:	ENJOYABLE ☆☆☆	

NOTES/PHOTOGRAPH/KEEP SAKE:

_____

_____

_____

_____

_____

_____

_____

_____

_____

_____

_____

_____

_____

_____

BEINN CHABHAIR

"THE HILL OF THE HAWK"

LOCH LOMOND		933M

DATE:	DISTANCE:	
WEATHER:	PEE	POO
TIME TAKEN:	ENJOYABLE ☆☆☆	

NOTES/PHOTOGRAPH/KEEP SAKE:

_____
_____
_____
_____
_____
_____
_____
_____
_____
_____
_____
_____
_____

BEINN IME

"THE HILL OF BUTTER"

LOCH LOMOND		1011M
DATE:	DISTANCE:	
WEATHER:	PEE	POO
TIME TAKEN:	ENJOYABLE ☆☆☆	

NOTES/PHOTOGRAPH/KEEP SAKE:

_____
_____
_____
_____
_____
_____
_____
_____
_____
_____
_____
_____
_____
_____

BEINN NARNAIN

"THE HILL OF NOTCHES"

LOCH LOMOND   926M

DATE:	DISTANCE:	
WEATHER:	PEE	POO
TIME TAKEN:	ENJOYABLE ☆☆☆	

NOTES/PHOTOGRAPH/KEEP SAKE:

_____
_____
_____
_____
_____
_____
_____
_____
_____
_____
_____
_____
_____

BEINN TULAICHEAN
"THE MOUNTAIN OF HILLOCKS"

LOCH LOMOND		946M

DATE:	DISTANCE:	
WEATHER:	PEE	POO
TIME TAKEN:	ENLOYABLE ☆☆☆	

NOTES/PHOTOGRAPH/KEEP SAKE:

_____
_____
_____
_____
_____
_____
_____
_____
_____
_____
_____
_____
_____
_____

BEN LOMOND

"THE BEACON MOUNTAIN"

LOCH LOMOND	974M

DATE:	DISTANCE:

WEATHER:	PEE	POO

TIME TAKEN:	ENJOYABLE ☆☆☆

NOTES/PHOTOGRAPH/KEEP SAKE:

_____
_____
_____
_____
_____
_____
_____
_____
_____
_____
_____
_____
_____
_____

BEN MORE
"THE BIG MOUNTAIN"

LOCH LOMOND		1174M	
DATE:	**DISTANCE:**		
WEATHER:	**PEE**		**POO**
TIME TAKEN:	**ENJOYABLE** ☆☆☆		

NOTES/PHOTOGRAPH/KEEP SAKE:

_____
_____
_____
_____
_____
_____
_____
_____
_____
_____
_____
_____
_____
_____

BEN VANE

"THE MIDDLE MOUNTAIN"

LOCH LOMOND	915M

DATE:	DISTANCE:	
WEATHER:	PEE	POO
TIME TAKEN:	ENJOYABLE ☆☆☆	

NOTES/PHOTOGRAPH/KEEP SAKE:

_____
_____
_____
_____
_____
_____
_____
_____
_____
_____
_____
_____
_____
_____

BEN VORLICH (LOCH LOMOND)

"THE HILL OF THE BAY"

LOCH LOMOND   943M

DATE:	DISTANCE:	
WEATHER:	PEE	POO
TIME TAKEN:	ENJOYABLE ☆☆☆	

NOTES/PHOTOGRAPH/KEEP SAKE:

_____
_____
_____
_____
_____
_____
_____
_____
_____
_____
_____
_____
_____

CRUACH ARDRAIN

"THE STACK OF THE HIGH PART"

LOCH LOMOND	1046M

DATE:	DISTANCE:	
WEATHER:	PEE	POO
TIME TAKEN:	ENJOYABLE ☆☆☆	

NOTES/PHOTOGRAPH/KEEP SAKE:

_____

_____

_____

_____

_____

_____

_____

_____

_____

_____

_____

_____

_____

MEALL GLAS

"THE ROUNDED GREEN HILL"

LOCH LOMOND		959M

DATE:	DISTANCE:	
WEATHER:	PEE	POO
TIME TAKEN:	ENJOYABLE ☆☆☆	

NOTES/PHOTOGRAPH/KEEP SAKE:

_____

_____

_____

_____

_____

_____

_____

_____

_____

_____

_____

_____

_____

_____

SGIATH CHUIL
"THE BACK WING"

LOCH LOMOND	921M

DATE:	DISTANCE:		
WEATHER:		PEE	POO
TIME TAKEN:	ENJOYABLE ☆☆☆		

NOTES/PHOTOGRAPH/KEEP SAKE:

_____
_____
_____
_____
_____
_____
_____
_____
_____
_____
_____
_____
_____
_____

STOB BINNEIN

"THE CONICAL PEAK"

LOCH LOMOND		1165M	
DATE:	DISTANCE:		
WEATHER:		PEE	POO
TIME TAKEN:	ENJOYABLE ☆ ☆ ☆		

NOTES/PHOTOGRAPH/KEEP SAKE:

_____
_____
_____
_____
_____
_____
_____
_____
_____
_____
_____
_____
_____
_____

AN RIABHACHAN

"THE STREAKED ONE"

LOCH NESS	1129M

DATE:	DISTANCE:

WEATHER:	PEE	POO

TIME TAKEN:	ENJOYABLE ☆☆☆

NOTES/PHOTOGRAPH/KEEP SAKE:

_____

_____

_____

_____

_____

_____

_____

_____

_____

_____

_____

_____

_____

_____

AN SOCACH (AFFRIC)

"THE SNOUT"

LOCH NESS	921M

DATE:	DISTANCE:	
WEATHER:	PEE	POO
TIME TAKEN:	ENJOYABLE ☆☆☆	

NOTES/PHOTOGRAPH/KEEP SAKE:

_____
_____
_____
_____
_____
_____
_____
_____
_____
_____
_____
_____
_____
_____

AN SOCACH (MULLARDOCH)

"THE SNOUT"

LOCH NESS	1069M

DATE:	DISTANCE:

WEATHER:	PEE	POO

TIME TAKEN:	ENJOYABLE ☆☆☆

NOTES/PHOTOGRAPH/KEEP SAKE:

_____
_____
_____
_____
_____
_____
_____
_____
_____
_____
_____
_____
_____

BEINN FHIONNLAIDH (CARN EIGE)

"THE FINDLAY'S HILL"

LOCH NESS   1005M

DATE:	DISTANCE:	
WEATHER:	PEE	POO
TIME TAKEN:	ENJOYABLE ☆☆☆	

NOTES/PHOTOGRAPH/KEEP SAKE:

_____
_____
_____
_____
_____
_____
_____
_____
_____
_____
_____
_____
_____
_____

BEN WYVIS

"THE HILL OF TERROR"

LOCH NESS	1046M

DATE:	DISTANCE:	
WEATHER:	PEE	POO
TIME TAKEN:	**ENJOYABLE** ☆☆☆	

NOTES/PHOTOGRAPH/KEEP SAKE:

_____

_____

_____

_____

_____

_____

_____

_____

_____

_____

_____

_____

CARN EIGE

"THE NOTCH HILL"

LOCH NESS   1183M

DATE:	DISTANCE:	
WEATHER:	PEE	POO
TIME TAKEN:	ENJOYABLE ☆☆☆	

NOTES/PHOTOGRAPH/KEEP SAKE:

_____
_____
_____
_____
_____
_____
_____
_____
_____
_____
_____
_____
_____
_____

CARN NAN GOBHAR (LOCH MULLARDOCH)

"THE CAIRN LIKE HILL OF THE GOATS"

LOCH NESS   992M

DATE:	DISTANCE:		
WEATHER:		PEE	POO
TIME TAKEN:	ENJOYABLE ☆☆☆		

NOTES/PHOTOGRAPH/KEEP SAKE:

_____
_____
_____
_____
_____
_____
_____
_____
_____
_____
_____
_____
_____
_____

CARN NAN GOBHAR (STRATHFARRAR)

"THE CAIRN LIKE HILL OF THE GOATS"

LOCH NESS 992M

DATE:	DISTANCE:	
WEATHER:	PEE	POO
TIME TAKEN:	ENJOYABLE ☆☆☆	

NOTES/PHOTOGRAPH/KEEP SAKE:

_____
_____
_____
_____
_____
_____
_____
_____
_____
_____
_____
_____
_____
_____

MAM SODHAIL

"THE LARGE ROUNDED HILL OF THE BARN"

LOCH NESS   1181M

DATE:	DISTANCE:	
WEATHER:	PEE	POO
TIME TAKEN:	ENJOYABLE ☆☆☆	

NOTES/PHOTOGRAPH/KEEP SAKE:

_____

_____

_____

_____

_____

_____

_____

_____

_____

_____

_____

_____

_____

MULLACH NAN DHEIRAGAIN

"THE SUMMIT OF THE HAWKS"

LOCH NESS	982M

DATE:	DISTANCE:	
WEATHER:	PEE	POO
TIME TAKEN:	**ENJOYABLE** ☆☆☆	

NOTES/PHOTOGRAPH/KEEP SAKE:

_____

_____

_____

_____

_____

_____

_____

_____

_____

_____

_____

_____

_____

SGURR A'CHOIRE GHLAIS

"THE ROCKY PEAK OF THE GREY CORRIE"

LOCH NESS	1083M

DATE:	DISTANCE:

WEATHER:	PEE	POO

TIME TAKEN:	ENJOYABLE ☆ ☆ ☆

NOTES/PHOTOGRAPH/KEEP SAKE:

_____
_____
_____
_____
_____
_____
_____
_____
_____
_____
_____
_____
_____

SGURR FHUAR-THUILL

"THE ROCKY PEAK OF THE COLD HOLLOW"

LOCH NESS	1049M

DATE:	DISTANCE:	
WEATHER:	PEE	POO
TIME TAKEN:	ENJOYABLE ☆☆☆	

NOTES/PHOTOGRAPH/KEEP SAKE:

_____

_____

_____

_____

_____

_____

_____

_____

_____

_____

_____

_____

_____

SGURR NA LAPAICH

"THE ROCKY PEAK OF THE BOG"

| LOCH NESS | 1150M |

DATE:	DISTANCE:	
WEATHER:	PEE	POO
TIME TAKEN:	ENJOYABLE ☆☆☆	

NOTES/PHOTOGRAPH/KEEP SAKE:

_____
_____
_____
_____
_____
_____
_____
_____
_____
_____
_____
_____
_____

SGURR NA RUAIDHE

"THE ROCKY PEAK OF REDNESS"

LOCH NESS	993M

DATE:	DISTANCE:	
WEATHER:	PEE	POO
TIME TAKEN:	ENJOYABLE ☆☆☆	

NOTES/PHOTOGRAPH/KEEP SAKE:

_____

_____

_____

_____

_____

_____

_____

_____

_____

_____

_____

_____

_____

SGURR NAN CEATHREAMHNAN

"THE ROCKY PEAK OF THE QUARTERS"

LOCH NESS   1151M

DATE:	DISTANCE:	
WEATHER:	PEE	POO
TIME TAKEN:	ENJOYABLE ☆☆☆	

NOTES/PHOTOGRAPH/KEEP SAKE:

_____

_____

_____

_____

_____

_____

_____

_____

_____

_____

_____

_____

_____

TOLL CREAGACH

"THE ROCKY HOLLOW"

LOCH NESS   1054M

DATE:	DISTANCE:	
WEATHER:	PEE	POO
TIME TAKEN:	ENJOYABLE ☆☆☆	

NOTES/PHOTOGRAPH/KEEP SAKE:

_____
_____
_____
_____
_____
_____
_____
_____
_____
_____
_____
_____
_____
_____

TOM A'CHOINICH

"THE HILL OF THE MOSS"

LOCH NESS	1112M

DATE:	DISTANCE:	
WEATHER:	PEE	POO
TIME TAKEN:	ENJOYABLE ☆☆☆	

NOTES/PHOTOGRAPH/KEEP SAKE:

_____

_____

_____

_____

_____

_____

_____

_____

_____

_____

_____

_____

_____

_____

AN STUC
"THE STEEP HILL"

PERTHSHIRE	1118M

DATE:	DISTANCE:	
WEATHER:	PEE	POO
TIME TAKEN:	ENJOYABLE ☆☆☆	

NOTES/PHOTOGRAPH/KEEP SAKE:

_____

_____

_____

_____

_____

_____

_____

_____

_____

_____

_____

_____

_____

BEINN DEARG (BLAIR ATHOLL)

"THE RED HILL"

PERTHSHIRE　　　　1008M

DATE:	DISTANCE:		
WEATHER:		PEE	POO
TIME TAKEN:	ENJOYABLE ☆☆☆		

NOTES/PHOTOGRAPH/KEEP SAKE:

_____
_____
_____
_____
_____
_____
_____
_____
_____
_____
_____
_____
_____

BEINN GHLAS
"THE GREEN HILL"

PERTHSHIRE	1103M

DATE:	DISTANCE:	
WEATHER:	PEE	POO
TIME TAKEN:	ENJOYABLE ☆☆☆	

NOTES/PHOTOGRAPH/KEEP SAKE:

_____
_____
_____
_____
_____
_____
_____
_____
_____
_____
_____
_____
_____
_____
_____

BEINN HEASGARNICH

"THE PEACEFUL HILL"

PERTHSHIRE	1078M

DATE:	DISTANCE:	
WEATHER:	PEE	POO
TIME TAKEN:	ENJOYABLE ☆☆☆	

NOTES/PHOTOGRAPH/KEEP SAKE:

_____
_____
_____
_____
_____
_____
_____
_____
_____
_____
_____
_____
_____

BEN CHONZIE

"THE MOUNTAIN OF THE MOSS"

PERTHSHIRE	931M

DATE:	DISTANCE:	
WEATHER:	PEE	POO
TIME TAKEN:	ENJOYABLE ☆☆☆	

NOTES/PHOTOGRAPH/KEEP SAKE:

_____
_____
_____
_____
_____
_____
_____
_____
_____
_____
_____
_____
_____
_____

BEN LAWERS

"THE HILL OF THE LOUD STREAM"

PERTHSHIRE	1214M

DATE:	DISTANCE:

WEATHER:	PEE	POO

TIME TAKEN:	ENJOYABLE ☆☆☆

NOTES/PHOTOGRAPH/KEEP SAKE:

_____
_____
_____
_____
_____
_____
_____
_____
_____
_____
_____
_____
_____

BEN VORLICH (LOCH EARN)

"THE HILL OF THE BAY"

PERTHSHIRE	985M

DATE:	DISTANCE:	
WEATHER:	PEE	POO
TIME TAKEN:	ENJOYABLE ☆☆☆	

NOTES/PHOTOGRAPH/KEEP SAKE:

_____

_____

_____

_____

_____

_____

_____

_____

_____

_____

_____

_____

_____

BRAIGH COIRE CHRUINN-BHALGAIN

"THE HEIGHT OF THE CORRIE OF THE ROUND LUMPS"

PERTHSHIRE   **1070M**

DATE:	DISTANCE:	
WEATHER:	**PEE**	**POO**

TIME TAKEN:	ENJOYABLE ☆☆☆

NOTES/PHOTOGRAPH/KEEP SAKE:

_____
_____
_____
_____
_____
_____
_____
_____
_____
_____
_____
_____
_____
_____

CARN A'CHLAMAIN

"THE CAIRN LIKE PEAK OF THE BUZZARD"

PERTHSHIRE	963M

DATE:	DISTANCE:	
WEATHER:	PEE	POO
TIME TAKEN:	ENJOYABLE ☆☆☆	

NOTES/PHOTOGRAPH/KEEP SAKE:

_____
_____
_____
_____
_____
_____
_____
_____
_____
_____
_____
_____
_____
_____

CARN AN RIGH

"THE HILL OF THE KING"

PERTHSHIRE	1029M

DATE:	DISTANCE:

WEATHER:	PEE	POO

TIME TAKEN:	ENJOYABLE ☆☆☆

NOTES/PHOTOGRAPH/KEEP SAKE:

_____
_____
_____
_____
_____
_____
_____
_____
_____
_____
_____
_____
_____

CARN GORM

"THE BLUE CAIRN SHAPED HIL"

PERTHSHIRE   1029M

DATE:	DISTANCE:	
WEATHER:	PEE	POO
TIME TAKEN:	**ENJOYABLE** ☆☆☆	

NOTES/PHOTOGRAPH/KEEP SAKE:

_____

_____

_____

_____

_____

_____

_____

_____

_____

_____

_____

_____

_____

CARN LIATH (BEINN A'GHLO)

"THE GREY PEAK"

PERTHSHIRE	975M

DATE:	DISTANCE:		
WEATHER:	PEE		POO
TIME TAKEN:	ENJOYABLE ☆☆☆		

NOTES/PHOTOGRAPH/KEEP SAKE:

_____

_____

_____

_____

_____

_____

_____

_____

_____

_____

_____

_____

_____

CARN MAIRG
"THE HILL OF SORROW"

PERTHSHIRE	1042M

DATE:	DISTANCE:	

WEATHER:	PEE	POO

TIME TAKEN:

ENJOYABLE

☆ ☆ ☆

NOTES/PHOTOGRAPH/KEEP SAKE:

_____

_____

_____

_____

_____

_____

_____

_____

_____

_____

_____

_____

CARN NAN GABHAR

"THE PEAK OF THE GOATS"

PERTHSHIRE   1121M

DATE:	DISTANCE:	
WEATHER:	PEE	POO
TIME TAKEN:	ENJOYABLE ☆☆☆	

NOTES/PHOTOGRAPH/KEEP SAKE:

_____

_____

_____

_____

_____

_____

_____

_____

_____

_____

_____

_____

_____

CREAG MHOR (GLEN LOCHAY)

"THE BIG CRAG"

PERTHSHIRE		1047M

DATE:	DISTANCE:	
WEATHER:	PEE	POO
TIME TAKEN:	ENJOYABLE ☆ ☆ ☆	

NOTES/PHOTOGRAPH/KEEP SAKE:

_____

_____

_____

_____

_____

_____

_____

_____

_____

_____

_____

_____

CREAG MHOR (MEALL NA AIGHEAN)

"THE BIG CRAG"

PERTHSHIRE   981M

DATE:	DISTANCE:	
WEATHER:	PEE	POO
TIME TAKEN:	**ENJOYABLE** ☆☆☆	

NOTES/PHOTOGRAPH/KEEP SAKE:

_____

_____

_____

_____

_____

_____

_____

_____

_____

_____

_____

_____

_____

_____

GLAS TULAICHEAN

"THE GREEN-GREY HILLOCKS"

PERTHSHIRE	1051M

DATE:	DISTANCE:	
WEATHER:	**PEE**	**POO**
TIME TAKEN:	**ENJOYABLE** ☆☆☆	

NOTES/PHOTOGRAPH/KEEP SAKE:

_____
_____
_____
_____
_____
_____
_____
_____
_____
_____
_____
_____
_____
_____

MEALL A'CHOIRE LEITH

"THE HILL OF THE GREY CORRIE"

PERTHSHIRE	926M

DATE:	DISTANCE:	
WEATHER:	PEE	POO
TIME TAKEN:	ENJOYABLE ☆☆☆	

NOTES/PHOTOGRAPH/KEEP SAKE:

_____

_____

_____

_____

_____

_____

_____

_____

_____

_____

_____

_____

_____

MEALL BUIDHE (GLEN LYON)

"THE YELLOW HILL"

PERTHSHIRE   932M

DATE:	DISTANCE:	
WEATHER:	PEE	POO
TIME TAKEN:	**ENJOYABLE** ☆☆☆	

NOTES/PHOTOGRAPH/KEEP SAKE:

_____
_____
_____
_____
_____
_____
_____
_____
_____
_____
_____
_____
_____
_____

MEALL CORRANAICH

"THE HILL OF LAMENT"

PERTHSHIRE   1069M

DATE:	DISTANCE:	

WEATHER:	PEE	POO

TIME TAKEN:	ENJOYABLE ☆☆☆

NOTES/PHOTOGRAPH/KEEP SAKE:

_____

_____

_____

_____

_____

_____

_____

_____

_____

_____

_____

_____

_____

MEALL GARBH (BEN LAWERS)

"THE ROUNDED ROUGH HILL"

PERTHSHIRE		1118M

DATE:	DISTANCE:	
WEATHER:	**PEE**	**POO**
TIME TAKEN:	**ENJOYABLE** ☆ ☆ ☆	

NOTES/PHOTOGRAPH/KEEP SAKE:

_____
_____
_____
_____
_____
_____
_____
_____
_____
_____
_____
_____
_____
_____

MEALL GARBH (CARN MAIRG)

"THE ROUNDED ROUGH HILL"

PERTHSHIRE	968M

DATE:	DISTANCE:	
WEATHER:	PEE	POO
TIME TAKEN:	ENJOYABLE ☆☆☆	

NOTES/PHOTOGRAPH/KEEP SAKE:

_____

_____

_____

_____

_____

_____

_____

_____

_____

_____

_____

_____

MEALL GHAORDAIDH

"THE HILL OF THE SHOULDER"

PERTHSHIRE	1039M

DATE:	DISTANCE:	
WEATHER:	PEE	POO
TIME TAKEN:	ENJOYABLE ☆☆☆	

NOTES/PHOTOGRAPH/KEEP SAKE:

_____
_____
_____
_____
_____
_____
_____
_____
_____
_____
_____
_____
_____
_____

MEALL GREIGH

"THE HILL OF THE HORSE STUDS"

PERTHSHIRE	1001M

DATE:	DISTANCE:

WEATHER:	PEE	POO

TIME TAKEN:	ENJOYABLE ☆ ☆ ☆

NOTES/PHOTOGRAPH/KEEP SAKE:

_____

_____

_____

_____

_____

_____

_____

_____

_____

_____

_____

_____

_____

MEALL NAN TARMACHAN
"THE HILL OF THE PTARMIGAN"

PERTHSHIRE		1044M

DATE:	DISTANCE:	
WEATHER:	PEE	POO
TIME TAKEN:	ENJOYABLE ☆☆☆	

NOTES/PHOTOGRAPH/KEEP SAKE:

_____
_____
_____
_____
_____
_____
_____
_____
_____
_____
_____
_____
_____
_____

SCHIEHALLION

"THE FAIRY HILL OF THE CALEDONIANS"

PERTHSHIRE	1083M

DATE:	DISTANCE:	
WEATHER:	PEE	POO
TIME TAKEN:	ENJOYABLE ☆☆☆	

NOTES/PHOTOGRAPH/KEEP SAKE:

_____

_____

_____

_____

_____

_____

_____

_____

_____

_____

_____

STUC A'CHROIN

"THE PEAK OF THE DANGER"

PERTHSHIRE		975M
DATE:	DISTANCE:	
WEATHER:	PEE	POO
TIME TAKEN:	ENJOYABLE ☆☆☆	

NOTES/PHOTOGRAPH/KEEP SAKE:

_____
_____
_____
_____
_____
_____
_____
_____
_____
_____
_____
_____
_____
_____

STUCHD AN LOCHAIN

"THE PEAK OF THE LITTLE LOCH"

PERTHSHIRE	960M

DATE:	DISTANCE:		
WEATHER:	PEE		POO
TIME TAKEN:	ENJOYABLE ☆☆☆		

NOTES/PHOTOGRAPH/KEEP SAKE:

_____

_____

_____

_____

_____

_____

_____

_____

_____

_____

_____

_____

_____

BEN HOPE

"THE MOUNTAIN OF THE BAY"

SUTHERLAND	927M

DATE:	DISTANCE:	
WEATHER:	PEE	POO
TIME TAKEN:	ENJOYABLE ☆☆☆	

NOTES/PHOTOGRAPH/KEEP SAKE:

_____

_____

_____

_____

_____

_____

_____

_____

_____

_____

_____

_____

_____

_____

BEN KLIBRECK

"THE HILL OH THE SPECKLED CLIFF"

SUTHERLAND	961M

DATE:	DISTANCE:

WEATHER:	PEE	POO

TIME TAKEN:	ENJOYABLE ☆☆☆

NOTES/PHOTOGRAPH/KEEP SAKE:

_____

_____

_____

_____

_____

_____

_____

_____

_____

_____

_____

_____

_____

BEINN LIATH MHOR

"THE BIG GREY HILL"

TORRIDON		926M

DATE:	DISTANCE:	
WEATHER:	PEE	POO
TIME TAKEN:	**ENJOYABLE** ☆☆☆	

NOTES/PHOTOGRAPH/KEEP SAKE:

_____
_____
_____
_____
_____
_____
_____
_____
_____
_____
_____
_____
_____
_____
_____

BIDEIN A'CHOIRE SHEASGAICH

"THE SUMMIT OF THE CORRIE OF THE FALLOW CATTLE"

DATE:	DISTANCE:	
WEATHER:	PEE	POO
TIME TAKEN:	ENJOYABLE ☆☆☆	

NOTES/PHOTOGRAPH/KEEP SAKE:

_____
_____
_____
_____
_____
_____
_____
_____
_____
_____
_____
_____
_____
_____

FIONN BHEINN

"THE WHITE HILL"

TORRIDON		933M

DATE:	DISTANCE:	
WEATHER:	PEE	POO
TIME TAKEN:	ENJOYABLE ☆☆☆	

NOTES/PHOTOGRAPH/KEEP SAKE:

_____
_____
_____
_____
_____
_____
_____
_____
_____
_____
_____
_____
_____
_____
_____

LURG MHOR

"THE BIG RIDGE"

TORRIDON	986M

DATE:	DISTANCE:	
WEATHER:	PEE	POO
TIME TAKEN:	**ENJOYABLE** ☆ ☆ ☆	

NOTES/PHOTOGRAPH/KEEP SAKE:

_____

_____

_____

_____

_____

_____

_____

_____

_____

_____

_____

_____

_____

MAOILE LUNNDAIDH

"THE BARE WET HILL"

TORRIDON	1007M

DATE:	DISTANCE:	
WEATHER:	PEE	POO
TIME TAKEN:	ENJOYABLE ☆☆☆	

NOTES/PHOTOGRAPH/KEEP SAKE:

_____
_____
_____
_____
_____
_____
_____
_____
_____
_____
_____
_____
_____
_____
_____
_____

MAOL CHEAN-DEARG

"THE BALD RED HEAD"

TORRIDON	933M

DATE:	DISTANCE:	
WEATHER:	PEE	POO
TIME TAKEN:	ENJOYABLE ☆ ☆ ☆	

NOTES/PHOTOGRAPH/KEEP SAKE:

_____
_____
_____
_____
_____
_____
_____
_____
_____
_____
_____
_____
_____

MORUISG
"THE BIG WATER"

TORRIDON		928M

DATE:	DISTANCE:	
WEATHER:	PEE	POO
TIME TAKEN:	ENJOYABLE ☆☆☆	

NOTES/PHOTOGRAPH/KEEP SAKE:

_____

_____

_____

_____

_____

_____

_____

_____

_____

_____

_____

_____

_____

_____

MULLACH AN RATHAIN (LIATHACH)

"THE BALD RED HEAD"

TORRIDON	1023M

DATE:	DISTANCE:

WEATHER:	PEE	POO

TIME TAKEN:	ENJOYABLE ☆☆☆

NOTES/PHOTOGRAPH/KEEP SAKE:

_____
_____
_____
_____
_____
_____
_____
_____
_____
_____
_____
_____
_____

RUADH-STAC MOR (BEINN EIGHE)
"THE BIG RED STACK"

TORRIDON	1010M

DATE:	DISTANCE:	
WEATHER:	PEE	POO
TIME TAKEN:	ENJOYABLE ☆☆☆	

NOTES/PHOTOGRAPH/KEEP SAKE:

_____
_____
_____
_____
_____
_____
_____
_____
_____
_____
_____
_____
_____
_____

SGORR RUADH

"THE RED ROCKY PEAK"

TORRIDON	962M

DATE:	DISTANCE:	
WEATHER:	PEE	POO
TIME TAKEN:	**ENJOYABLE** ☆☆☆	

NOTES/PHOTOGRAPH/KEEP SAKE:

_____

_____

_____

_____

_____

_____

_____

_____

_____

_____

_____

_____

_____

SGURR A'CHAORACHAIN

"THE PEAK OF THE LITTLE BERRY FIELD"

TORRIDON	1053M

DATE:	DISTANCE:	
WEATHER:	PEE	POO
TIME TAKEN:	ENJOYABLE ☆☆☆	

NOTES/PHOTOGRAPH/KEEP SAKE:

_____
_____
_____
_____
_____
_____
_____
_____
_____
_____
_____
_____
_____
_____
_____

SGURR CHOINNICH

"THE ROCKY PEAK OF THE MOSS"

TORRIDON	999M

DATE:	DISTANCE:	

WEATHER:	PEE	POO

TIME TAKEN:	ENJOYABLE ☆☆☆

NOTES/PHOTOGRAPH/KEEP SAKE:

_____
_____
_____
_____
_____
_____
_____
_____
_____
_____
_____
_____
_____

SGURR MOR (BEINN ALLIGIN)

"THE BIG PEAK"

TORRIDON	986M

DATE:	DISTANCE:	
WEATHER:	PEE	POO
TIME TAKEN:	ENJOYABLE ☆☆☆	

NOTES/PHOTOGRAPH/KEEP SAKE:

_____
_____
_____
_____
_____
_____
_____
_____
_____
_____
_____
_____
_____
_____
_____

SLIOCH

"THE SPEAR"

TORRIDON	981M

DATE:	DISTANCE:	
WEATHER:	PEE	POO
TIME TAKEN:	ENJOYABLE ☆☆☆	

NOTES/PHOTOGRAPH/KEEP SAKE:

_____

_____

_____

_____

_____

_____

_____

_____

_____

_____

_____

_____

_____

_____

SPIDEAN A'CHOIRE LEITH (LIATHACH)

"THE PEAK OF THE GREY CORRIE"

TORRIDON	1055M

DATE:	DISTANCE:	
WEATHER:	PEE	POO
TIME TAKEN:	ENJOYABLE ☆☆☆	

NOTES/PHOTOGRAPH/KEEP SAKE:

_____
_____
_____
_____
_____
_____
_____
_____
_____
_____
_____
_____
_____
_____

SPIDEAN COIRE NAN CLACH (BEINN EIGHE)

"THE PEAK OF THE CORRIE OF STONES"

TORRIDON	993M

DATE:	DISTANCE:	
WEATHER:	PEE	POO
TIME TAKEN:	ENJOYABLE ☆☆☆	

NOTES/PHOTOGRAPH/KEEP SAKE:

_____

_____

_____

_____

_____

_____

_____

_____

_____

_____

_____

_____

_____

TOM NA GRUAGAICH   (BEINN ALLIGIN)
"THE ROUNDED HILL OF THE MAIDEN"

TORRIDON		922M

DATE:	DISTANCE:	
WEATHER:	PEE	POO
TIME TAKEN:	ENJOYABLE ☆☆☆	

NOTES/PHOTOGRAPH/KEEP SAKE:

_____
_____
_____
_____
_____
_____
_____
_____
_____
_____
_____
_____
_____
_____
_____

A' CHAILLEACH
"THE OLD WOMAN"

ULLAPOOL	997M

DATE:	DISTANCE:	
WEATHER:	PEE	POO
TIME TAKEN:	**ENJOYABLE** ☆ ☆ ☆	

NOTES/PHOTOGRAPH/KEEP SAKE:

_____
_____
_____
_____
_____
_____
_____
_____
_____
_____
_____
_____
_____
_____

A' MHAIGHDEAN

"THE MAIDEN"

ULLAPOOL		967M	
DATE:	DISTANCE:		
WEATHER:		PEE	POO
TIME TAKEN:	ENJOYABLE ☆☆☆		

NOTES/PHOTOGRAPH/KEEP SAKE:

_____
_____
_____
_____
_____
_____
_____
_____
_____
_____
_____
_____
_____
_____
_____

AM FAOCHAGACH

"THE HEATHERY PLACE"

ULLAPOOL	954M

DATE:	DISTANCE:	
WEATHER:	PEE	POO
TIME TAKEN:	ENJOYABLE ☆☆☆	

NOTES/PHOTOGRAPH/KEEP SAKE:

_____

_____

_____

_____

_____

_____

_____

_____

_____

_____

_____

_____

_____

AN COILEACHAN
"THE LITTLE COCK"

ULLAPOOL		923M

DATE:	DISTANCE:	
WEATHER:	PEE	POO
TIME TAKEN:	ENJOYABLE ☆☆☆	

NOTES/PHOTOGRAPH/KEEP SAKE:

_____
_____
_____
_____
_____
_____
_____
_____
_____
_____
_____
_____
_____
_____

BEINN DEARG (ULLAPOOL)
"THE RED HILL"

ULLAPOOL   1084M

DATE:	DISTANCE:	
WEATHER:	PEE	POO
TIME TAKEN:	ENJOYABLE ☆☆☆	

NOTES/PHOTOGRAPH/KEEP SAKE:
_____
_____
_____
_____
_____
_____
_____
_____
_____
_____
_____
_____
_____
_____

BEINN LIATH MHOR FANNAICH
"THE BIG GREY HILL OF FANNAICH"

ULLAPOOL		954M

DATE:	DISTANCE:	
WEATHER:	PEE	POO
TIME TAKEN:	ENJOYABLE ☆☆☆	

NOTES/PHOTOGRAPH/KEEP SAKE:

_____
_____
_____
_____
_____
_____
_____
_____
_____
_____
_____
_____
_____
_____

BEINN TARSUINN

"THE TRANSVERSE HIL"

ULLAPOOL	937M

DATE:	DISTANCE:		
WEATHER:	PEE		POO
TIME TAKEN:	ENJOYABLE ☆☆☆		

NOTES/PHOTOGRAPH/KEEP SAKE:

_____
_____
_____
_____
_____
_____
_____
_____
_____
_____
_____
_____
_____
_____

BEN MORE ASSYNT

"THE BIG HILL OF THE ROCKY RIDGE"

ULLAPOOL	998M

DATE:	DISTANCE:	
WEATHER:	PEE	POO
TIME TAKEN:	ENJOYABLE ☆☆☆	

NOTES/PHOTOGRAPH/KEEP SAKE:

_____
_____
_____
_____
_____
_____
_____
_____
_____
_____
_____
_____
_____
_____

BIDEIN A'GHLAS THUILL (AN TEALLACH)

"THE PINNACLE OF THE GREEN HOLLOW"

ULLAPOOL	1062M

DATE:	DISTANCE:	
WEATHER:	PEE	POO
TIME TAKEN:	ENJOYABLE ☆☆☆	

NOTES/PHOTOGRAPH/KEEP SAKE:

_____
_____
_____
_____
_____
_____
_____
_____
_____
_____
_____
_____
_____

CONA' MHEALL
"THE ADJOINING HILL"

ULLAPOOL		978M

DATE:	DISTANCE:	
WEATHER:	PEE	POO
TIME TAKEN:	ENJOYABLE ☆☆☆	

NOTES/PHOTOGRAPH/KEEP SAKE:

_____
_____
_____
_____
_____
_____
_____
_____
_____
_____
_____
_____
_____
_____
_____
_____
_____

CONIVAL

"THE ADJOINING HILL"(from CONA'MHEALL)

ULLAPOOL	987M

DATE:	DISTANCE:	
WEATHER:	PEE	POO
TIME TAKEN:	ENJOYABLE ☆☆☆	

NOTES/PHOTOGRAPH/KEEP SAKE:

_____
_____
_____
_____
_____
_____
_____
_____
_____
_____
_____
_____
_____

EIDIDH NAN CLACH GEALA

"THE WEB OF THE WHITE STONES"

ULLAPOOL	927M

DATE:	DISTANCE:	
WEATHER:	PEE	POO
TIME TAKEN:	ENJOYABLE ☆☆☆	

NOTES/PHOTOGRAPH/KEEP SAKE:

_____

_____

_____

_____

_____

_____

_____

_____

_____

_____

_____

_____

_____

_____

MEALL A'CHRASGAIDH

"THE HILL OF THE CROSSING"

ULLAPOOL		934M

DATE:	DISTANCE:	
WEATHER:	**PEE**	**POO**
TIME TAKEN:	**ENJOYABLE** ☆☆☆	

NOTES/PHOTOGRAPH/KEEP SAKE:

_____

_____

_____

_____

_____

_____

_____

_____

_____

_____

_____

_____

_____

MEALL GORM

"THE BLUE ROUNDED HILL"

ULLAPOOL		949M

DATE:	DISTANCE:	
WEATHER:	PEE	POO
TIME TAKEN:	ENJOYABLE ☆ ☆ ☆	

NOTES/PHOTOGRAPH/KEEP SAKE:

_____
_____
_____
_____
_____
_____
_____
_____
_____
_____
_____
_____
_____
_____
_____

MEALL NAN CEAPRAICHEAN

"THE HILL OF THE STUBBY HILLOCKS"

ULLAPOOL	977M

DATE:	DISTANCE:

WEATHER:	PEE	POO

TIME TAKEN:	ENJOYABLE ☆ ☆ ☆

NOTES/PHOTOGRAPH/KEEP SAKE:

_____

_____

_____

_____

_____

_____

_____

_____

_____

_____

_____

_____

_____

_____

MULLACH COIRE MHIC FHEARCHAIR

"THE SUMMIT OF THE CORRIE OF MCFARQUAR"

ULLAPOOL	1019M

DATE:	DISTANCE:	
WEATHER:	PEE	POO
TIME TAKEN:	ENJOYABLE ☆☆☆	

NOTES/PHOTOGRAPH/KEEP SAKE:

_____
_____
_____
_____
_____
_____
_____
_____
_____
_____
_____
_____
_____
_____

RUADH STAC MOR

"THE BIG RED STACK"

ULLAPOOL	918M

DATE:	DISTANCE:	
WEATHER:	PEE	POO
TIME TAKEN:	ENJOYABLE ☆☆☆	

NOTES/PHOTOGRAPH/KEEP SAKE:

_____
_____
_____
_____
_____
_____
_____
_____
_____
_____
_____
_____
_____
_____

SEANA BHRAIGH

"THE OLD HEIGHT"

ULLAPOOL		926M	
DATE:	**DISTANCE:**		
WEATHER:		PEE	POO
TIME TAKEN:	**ENJOYABLE** ☆☆☆		

NOTES/PHOTOGRAPH/KEEP SAKE:

_____
_____
_____
_____
_____
_____
_____
_____
_____
_____
_____
_____
_____
_____
_____

SGURR BAN

"THE WHITE ROCKY PEAK"

ULLAPOOL	989M

DATE:	DISTANCE:

WEATHER:	PEE	POO

TIME TAKEN:	ENJOYABLE ☆ ☆ ☆

NOTES/PHOTOGRAPH/KEEP SAKE:

_____
_____
_____
_____
_____
_____
_____
_____
_____
_____
_____
_____
_____
_____

SGURR BREAC

"THE SPECKLED ROCKY PEAK"

ULLAPOOL		999M

DATE:	DISTANCE:	
WEATHER:	PEE	POO
TIME TAKEN:	ENJOYABLE ☆☆☆	

NOTES/PHOTOGRAPH/KEEP SAKE:

_____
_____
_____
_____
_____
_____
_____
_____
_____
_____
_____
_____
_____
_____

SGURR FIONA (AN TEALLACH)

"THE WHITE PEAK"

ULLAPOOL   1060M

DATE:	DISTANCE:		
WEATHER:		PEE	POO
TIME TAKEN:	ENJOYABLE ☆☆☆		

NOTES/PHOTOGRAPH/KEEP SAKE:

_____

_____

_____

_____

_____

_____

_____

_____

_____

_____

_____

_____

_____

_____

SGURR MOR

"THE BIG PEAK"

ULLAPOOL   1110M

DATE:	DISTANCE:	
WEATHER:	PEE	POO
TIME TAKEN:	ENJOYABLE ☆☆☆	

NOTES/PHOTOGRAPH/KEEP SAKE:

_____
_____
_____
_____
_____
_____
_____
_____
_____
_____
_____
_____
_____
_____
_____

SGURR NAN CLACH GEALA

"THE PEAK OF THE WHITE STONES"

ULLAPOOL	1093M

DATE:	DISTANCE:

WEATHER:	PEE	POO

TIME TAKEN:	ENJOYABLE ☆☆☆

NOTES/PHOTOGRAPH/KEEP SAKE:

_____

_____

_____

_____

_____

_____

_____

_____

_____

_____

_____

_____

_____

SGURR NAN EACH
"THE PEAK OF THE HORSES"

| ULLAPOOL | | 923M |

DATE:	DISTANCE:	
WEATHER:	PEE	POO
TIME TAKEN:	ENJOYABLE ☆☆☆	

NOTES/PHOTOGRAPH/KEEP SAKE:

_____
_____
_____
_____
_____
_____
_____
_____
_____
_____
_____
_____
_____
_____

Printed in Great Britain
by Amazon